African Americans and Standardized Tests

The Real Reason for Low Test Scores

Veda Jairrels, J.D., Ph.D.

African American Images

To my mother and father
and to the memory of Carlos Juan and
my grandmother, my Big Mama, Mrs. Leila Harris.

Table of Contents

Acknowledgments

There are several individuals I must thank regarding this book. First, I owe a debt of gratitude to the administration of Clark Atlanta University (CAU) for their support as I completed this project. Dr. James Young, CAU professor, gave much needed advice regarding publishers. Denise McBean, CAU administrative assistant, graciously provided support services in her spare time. Latonya Burkhalter, another CAU administrative assistant, provided her typing skills. Dr. Earle Clowney and Patrika Dill, CAU graduate student, proofread the manuscript.

I am grateful for my parents, Dr. C.W. and Juanita Jairrels, who have supported me in all of my endeavors. My brother, Attorney William Jairrels, offered his home to me as a writing retreat. Other family members such as my son, Hank, my aunt, Mrs. Bernice Dickerson, and my uncles, Dr. Charles and Benny Harris, offered their prayers, advice, and encouragement.

I also thank Karen E. Quinones Miller for her advice and Donna Marie Williams, editor. Their assistance was invaluable.

Last, but certainly not least, I offer a heartfelt thanks to Dr. Jawanza Kunjufu for establishing a publishing company that allowed me to have a voice. I deeply appreciate his vision and entrepreneurial spirit.

Preface

Are you the parent of a bright, inquisitive child who wants to become a doctor? Are you constantly seeking ways to enhance your child's education? Perhaps you're not concerned with having a doctor in the family, but as a conscientious parent, you want to ensure that your child has a sound education and becomes a productive citizen.

Are you a teacher who is trying to improve the academic achievement of your students? Do you believe that the standardized test scores of African Americans are misleading and do not adequately reflect their intellectual capacity? Are you surprised by the fact that some of the most diligent students in your class have some of the lowest standardized test scores? Are you wondering what you can do?

Perhaps you are a policymaker, responsible for developing programs that will uplift all of America. You know there is an achievement gap, and perhaps you are aware of various reasons given for the gap. Are you wondering what you can do to actually make a difference?

Maybe you are just a concerned citizen. You want to do your part to make America prosper.

This book was written for all of you. I only ask that you read, think, and at least consider acting on the recommendations.

Introduction:

Why African Americans Usually Score the Lowest on Standardized Tests (Just Keeping It Real)

African American students, as a group, usually (not always) score the lowest on standardized tests. I believe African Americans score the lowest on standardized tests that focus on verbal (reading) ability because of a lack of "long-term voluntary reading" (Marx, 2002, B10). Voluntary reading is also referred to as reading for pleasure or leisure. This emphasis on reading should begin at birth (i.e., parents reading to their infants). The amount of reading that children do in connection with school assignments is often not enough. Therefore, children must read above and beyond what is required for school.

When I tell African American parents about the importance of taking their children to the library, they sometimes reply, "My child has plenty of books at home." My unspoken response is, "No, you don't. You just think you do."

In this book, I present the research and offer recommendations as to what parents, teachers, policymakers, and concerned citizens can do to manifest change. More important, African American parents are given guidelines as to the quantity of reading that is necessary to improve their children's performance on standardized tests. After reading this book, African American parents will realize, I hope, that no, they don't have enough books at home and yes, the power to improve their children's performance on standardized tests is in their hands.

The information contained in this book isn't new. Programs promoted by former First Lady Laura Bush ("Start Kids Reading Early, 2002"), the National Basketball Association, and others have tried to emphasize the importance of reading. Even Black Entertainment Television (BET) featured an animated video, replete with the "n" word and profanity, titled "Read a Book" (Armah, 2007). Unfortunately, these programs and messages haven't connected with the African American community in a meaningful way.

Many African American parents do not understand the amount of reading their children must do in order to maximize their scores on standardized tests. They know that reading is important, but they do not know how important and critical it is for improving performance on standardized tests.

Sometimes it is not so much what you say, but how you say it. What is novel about this book is that I state my conclusions bluntly: Lack of early reading experiences and a lack of voluntary reading above and beyond the school curriculum detrimentally affect the performance of African American students on standardized tests. This book also emphasizes what African American parents can do for their children, as opposed to relying on others.

It is not my purpose to negate the importance of adequately funded schools and well-qualified teachers. Not all children, however, have access to the best schools.

According to a report by the Education Trust, states tend to provide less money per pupil in school districts that are low-income, linguistically diverse, or minority (Arroyo, 2008). In 21 states, less money was spent per pupil in school districts with a high minority student population than in those districts with fewer minority students. Therefore, in this book, I provide strategies to guide parents, regardless of their socioeconomic status or the quality of the child's school. I hope educators will read this book and incorporate some of the recommendations into their curricula as well.

This book was written with a focus on students who do not have disabilities. Students with special needs may require specialized academic interventions. Educators, however, have also recommended some of the strategies in this book for parents of children with disabilities (Chute, 2007).

To African Americans

Some of you may disagree with my thesis. You may believe that academic performance is dependent solely on school quality, and you don't believe that something as simple as increasing students' reading time could have a major impact. I understand. All I ask is that you read carefully and with an open mind.

You may also fear that I'm a self-hating African American trying to ingratiate myself with ultra conservatives for personal gain. I do fear that my book will be used by those antagonistic to African Americans to say, "See, it's their fault anyway." I am not the first person to express concern about racists using research for nefarious purposes. When one African American professor reviewed the effect of parenting styles on academic achievement, he faced the same dilemma and concluded, "We must not allow bigots to intimidate us into silence" (Ferguson, 2005, p. 3).

To Non-African Americans

Although I certainly hope that members of different ethnic groups will read and believe in this book, I feel compelled to warn you that you shouldn't use my book to start cocktail conversations with African Americans. I am afraid that some young, well-intentioned White teacher will quote sentences from my book out of context, thereby incurring the wrath of African American parents.

Please don't start conversations with, "Well, the real reason Black students don't...." Do not say, "Black people don't read." The latter statement is not true, and African Americans will be offended by it. Moreover, you will be viewed with suspicion and come across as a racist idiot. These are prickly matters, and unfortunately, there is general distrust along racial and ethnic lines (Fournier & Tompson, 2008; "Minorities Mistrustful," 2008). Accusations of racism are often made regarding the use of language, politics, education, and even entertainment. Later in the book, I will provide recommendations on how you can effectuate change on these matters within your community.

Now that I've laid out the ground rules, let's get started.

Chapter 1

Who Cares About Standardized Tests Anyway?

African American children and adults are often kept out of educational programs, schools, universities, and jobs because of low standardized test scores. Standardized test scores are used as indicators of academic quality, achievement, and knowledge. For example, one purpose of the No Child Left Behind Act is to improve the academic achievement of all students. To comply with the law, school districts use standardized tests to assess and provide evidence of academic achievement (Yell, 2006).

Standardized tests are sometimes used to determine bonus pay and cash awards for teachers and students. The Arkansas Advanced Initiative for Math and Science (AAIMS) identified 11 schools in Arkansas with poor Advanced Placement (AP) participation rates (Hermes, 2007). Students from those schools who score at least a 3 on the AP tests (which are standardized) and their teachers will receive cash awards.

The AAIMS also identified schools whose AP participation could be improved. Teachers at those schools will receive cash awards if more students "score well" (Hermes, 2007). Similar incentive programs regarding AP exams have been implemented in Texas and New Mexico (Jackson, 2007; Schmidt, 2007). In the New York City public schools, students are also being paid to achieve on standardized tests and more than $500,000 has already been distributed (Medina, 2008b).

Louisiana school officials recommended that standardized tests be used to determine bonus pay. The

Recovery School District, which operates 30 public schools in New Orleans, proposed a plan in which support staff, teachers, and principals would receive bonus pay if schools achieve certain test scores. The bonuses range from $1,500 to $5,000 (Associated Press, 2007).

In the New York City public schools, researchers are looking at teacher effectiveness at 140 schools by studying students' improvement on standardized test scores (Medina, 2008a). Some participating principals did not inform their teachers that they were being evaluated in this manner. Furthermore, school officials mentioned that they may use the data to make decisions regarding teacher pay and tenure. The teachers' union and politicians immediately resisted this idea ("Albany Fails Again," 2008). They also said that they may make the findings about individual teachers public.

In some school districts in Texas, students who pass the state mandated standardized tests are given days off from school. The students who do not pass receive more attention from teachers (Chavez, 2008).

The emphasis on standardized tests may, however, pose additional problems. Some teachers and other school personnel may be encouraged to cheat. In Florida, 50 school staff members were disciplined for cheating or making errors during test administration. Ten teachers in the 10 years prior to 2008 lost their teacher certification permanently (Kaczor, 2008).

Not all educators welcome the emphasis on standardized tests. A teacher in the state of Washington refused to administer the Washington Assessment of Student Learning because he deemed it emotionally and academically harmful to students. He received a nine day suspension without pay for his stand (James, 2008).

Who Cares About Standardized Tests Anyway?

Standardized tests such as the SAT and the American College Test (ACT) are used by colleges and universities for admissions purposes. Some researchers argue that highly selective universities place too much emphasis on college admission tests (Schmidt, 2008). In the case of home-schooled students, however, test scores provide a means by which universities can compare their academic achievement with other students. These students usually do not receive grades or recommendations from third parties, such as teachers. Therefore, in addition to the SAT and ACT, some colleges require home-schooled students to take at least two or more SAT II subject tests (Wasley, 2007).

Even college-bound athletes must receive certain scores on the SAT or ACT in order to play sports their freshman year and receive athletic scholarships. For Division I universities, a sliding scale is used and the higher the student's high school GPA in core courses, the lower the SAT/ACT requirement, and vice versa. A student with a 2.4 GPA in core courses would need an 860 on the Critical Reading and Mathematics sections of the SAT or an ACT sum score of 71. In Division II colleges, a student needs a combined SAT of 820 or an ACT sum score of 68 in order to meet academic eligibility requirements. A sliding scale is not used in Division II colleges (Guide for the College-Bound Student-Athlete, n.d.).

Educational institutions are not alone in using standardized test scores. For example, when recruits sign up to join the military, they take the Armed Services Vocational Aptitude Battery (ASVAB), which consists of standardized tests in eight areas, including word knowledge and paragraph comprehension (ASVAB Career Exploration Program, n.d.).

African Americans and Standardized Tests

A score derived from the reading and math subtests determines whether recruits are allowed to join their military branch of choice. The Air Force requires the highest score and the Army the lowest. The test scores also determine whether recruits can pursue their chosen careers once in the military (The ASVAB Explained, n.d.). More job opportunities are open to those with higher scores. Test scores can also affect pay, because enlistment bonuses are dependent on the military job.

Sometimes standardized tests must be passed in order to obtain certain jobs. In many states, teachers, regardless of how many degrees they have, cannot become certified unless they pass certain standardized tests. Most states have a standardized test as a component of the bar exam that lawyers must pass in order to receive a license to practice law. Applicants for the police force have to take civil service exams that often have a standardized reading comprehension section.

I assert that the gatekeeper approach to standardized testing is unwise, and I do not always support limitations based on test scores. There are others who agree with me. For example, educators, psychologists, and university administrators at Tufts University developed optional assessments to measure other characteristics, such as creativity, and have used them to supplement the traditional admissions procedure (Sternberg, 2007). This supplement increased the diversity of their entering freshman class. In fact, over 750 universities have some type of test optional policy (Perez, 2008).

Administrators at Northeastern University devised an alternative admissions process for students who are the first in their families to attend college and who have endured

4

substantial hardships. During the evaluation process, the students complete a personality inventory, are interviewed, and participate in role-playing exercises. Although these students averaged about 300 points below the median SAT score at Northeastern, more than half of the students in the first cohort had at least a B average after their freshman year (Hoover, 2007). Students who do not score well on standardized tests but perform well in the classroom are the types of students that many K-12 teachers have seen throughout their teaching careers.

The National Association for College Admission Counseling (NACAC) established the Commission on the Use of Standardized Tests in Undergraduate Admission. The commission is charged with exploring the use of testing for college admissions. This organization, like Sternberg (2007) and Northeastern University, is questioning what other types of assessments can be used to provide additional information about applicants. NACAC acknowledged in a report, however, that 60 percent of colleges surveyed responded that the ACT and SAT test results were "considerably important" (Farrell & Hoover, 2007, p. A 35).

Although I applaud the efforts of these institutions and hope others will follow suit, I remain a realist. At this time, I cannot stop the use of standardized tests, and I do believe they will be used for many years to come. Even if standardized tests were eliminated for college admissions, they would still probably exist for certain jobs and K–12 schools. Elementary and secondary schools have added many standardized tests to their academic program in the past two years ("Making a Profit," 2007). Therefore, increasing the scores of African American students on such tests is critical.

African Americans and Standardized Tests

African American children and adults should at least be able to earn scores that will not hinder them from achieving their educational and career goals. In addition, I believe in the power and value of reading for human development, even without its effect on standardized test scores (Cunningham & Stanovich, 1998; National Endowment for the Arts, 2007). Long-term reading beginning at birth (i.e., parents reading daily to their children) must become an integral part of the entire African American community.

Chapter 2

The African American Past and the Impact on Reading: From Africa to America

In order to discuss the literacy heritage of African Americans, it is necessary to return to the continent of our origin and explore the status of literacy there. Now the last thing I want to do is spread misinformation about Africa. According to John O. Hunwick, an African history scholar, many may think of Africa as a continent whose heritage is steeped in an oral tradition without books or reading (Castillo, 2002). There are, however, hundreds of thousands of written manuscripts in Africa that are centuries old. These manuscripts are written in Arabic, and some are written in African languages using Arabic lettering. Another scholar, Stephanie Diakite, stated that "when much of Europe was in its Dark Ages, Africa was recording its literate history" (Castillo, p. A26, 2002).

These scholars contend that many slaves brought to America were literate and that one of the earliest slave autobiographies was written in Arabic by a slave named Omar ibn Sayyid (Castillo, 2002). Obviously, this literacy in Arabic did not flourish among the slaves. There was no need for Arabic, nor the time or the means to teach it.

These same scholars also contend, however, that the majority of West Africans were illiterate, and I have found no evidence to suggest that a familial habit of reading developed throughout West Africa. I assume that at least some Africans who were illiterate were also enslaved and sent to America. Therefore, both Africans who were literate in Arabic and those

7

who were not literate at all found themselves living as slaves in a hostile and racist America.

What Happened in America?

Proponents of slavery advanced several arguments to support human bondage. Some argued that the African was intellectually and biological inferior, that slavery was necessary to spread Christianity to the savages, and that the slaves were needed for the economic development of the country (Franklin, & Moss, 2005). George Fitzhugh, a southern attorney and the son of a physician/planter, said that slavery prevented the "Negro" from becoming a burden on society and that freedom would be the Black man's curse (Fitzhugh, 1857). These theories certainly did nothing to promote the education of African slaves. The theories of Fitzhugh and others like him affected the slaves and their descendants in the areas of labor, civil rights, and education well into the 20th century. Indeed, some would argue these theories are still alive today.

In accordance with the belief system of those who supported slavery, as a general rule, slaves were not taught to read or write. In some states, educating slaves was against the law (McCague, 1972). Franklin and Moss (2005) contend, however, that these laws were routinely ignored by at least some slave owners in the South. Although the laws were effective, slaves violated the law at every opportunity (Author Q & A. n.d.). In the 1930s, John Field, a former slave, informed a Works Public Administration interviewer that the slaves wanted to learn to read and write, but any owner caught teaching a slave to read could be fined $50 and put in jail for a year (Home Box Office, 2002).

The African American Past and the Impact on Reading: From Africa to America

Even with the willingness of some slave owners to violate the law, becoming literate was an arduous task. For example, Frederick Douglass (1845) stated in his narrative that his mistress taught him the alphabet. Under orders from her husband, however, she ceased instruction. Her husband said, "If you teach that n— how to read, there would be no keeping him." After that, his mistress was determined to prevent any attempts at further education. If she saw him with a newspaper, she became enraged and closely watched him. Douglass then made friends with every White boy possible and persuaded them to teach him to read. He took bread from the house to share with poor White boys in exchange for their teaching him how to read.

Franklin and Moss (2005) quote an estimate that in Georgia, 5,000 out of 400,000 slaves were literate. If applied to slaves everywhere, that would mean approximately 1.25 percent of the slave population, or less than two slaves out of 100, were literate. Another estimate was that in 1865, 10 percent of African Americans in the South were literate (Fairclough, 2007). Clearly, given the legal restrictions and racist traditions and attitudes of the era, the majority of African Americans were illiterate. Slaves did not have the time or the means to engage in reading for pleasure.

After slavery ended, most African Americans remained in the South. Schools and libraries were not available to them. The schools that were available varied in quality. One historian who chronicled the conditions of these early schools noted that the Ku Klux Klan burned down schools and that White and Black teachers of African American students were sometimes harassed and murdered (Fairclough, 2007). Illiteracy was even a problem among teachers. In some schools, former Confederate soldiers served as teachers and some White teachers called their African American students the "n—" word, beat them, and made no effort to provide adequate instruction. According to Fairclough, education for many African Americans in the South remained virtually unchanged from 1870 to 1940.

The difficulty African Americans faced in obtaining an education in the first half of the 20th century is illustrated by the ordeal my parents experienced in their quest for education. My father was fortunate enough to attend a Rosenwald School in Randolph County, Alabama, which served students in the first through eighth grades.

Julius Rosenwald was a Jewish man who collaborated with Booker T. Washington to build schools for African Americans, using the concept of matching grants. African Americans in rural areas had to contribute financially, the local school board (White controlled, of course) had to agree to operate the school, and the Rosenwald Foundation usually paid one-fifth of the total cost of construction (Hanchett, n.d.). These schools were built in 15 states, which were Alabama, Arkansas, Florida, Georgia, Kentucky, Louisiana, Maryland, Mississippi, Missouri, North Carolina, Oklahoma, South Carolina, Tennessee, Texas, and Virginia (The Rosenwald Schools Initiative, n.d).

I am amazed that rural and often poor African Americans raised a total of $4.7 million to build primarily schools, workshops, and teacher housing. The Rosenwald Fund donated $4.3 million (Herbert S. Ford Museum, n.d.). These schools also received donations from concerned White community members and money from tax funds. In fact, officials gave a total $18.1 million from tax funds over the years for construction and upkeep of the schools (The Rosenwald Schools Initiative, n.d).

The African American Past and the Impact on Reading: From Africa to America

My great-grandfather agreed to donate the land for my father's school, and he and another man borrowed $600 to purchase the materials to build the school. The Randolph County School Board and the Rosenwald Foundation also gave $600 each for construction materials. In order to pay for labor costs, some of the African American men in the community, including my grandfather, donated $50 each. School construction was completed in 1920 (Randolph County Heritage Book Committee, 2000). The school did not have desks, but eventually the students built their own desks.

The acquisition of a high school education was even more difficult for my father and other African Americans. In Randolph County, there was only one high school for African Americans. This high school was located 29 miles from my father's home. Although there was bus transportation, the bus stop was located 12 miles from my father's home. My grandparents, like many African Americans of the time, did not have a car. Fortunately, my great-grandfather lived in the town where the school was located, and my father lived with him during the school year. African Americans who had no relatives in the town and who could not afford to board with families were just out of luck. If my father had been White, a bus would have picked him up at his home and driven him to the nearest high school for Whites, which was much closer to his home than the one for African Americans. Alabama never made an attempt to provide my father with a "separate but equal education."

My mother tells a similar story about her early education in rural Lee County, Alabama. The African American community built her elementary school, which went to the sixth grade. My mother and her siblings walked approximately three miles to school. They did not have desks and sat on benches. The school year for African American children was about four months, from November through February. White students who lived in the same area had bus transportation and a school year at least twice as long as their African American counterparts.

Lee County Training School served students in the first through twelfth grades. It was located about six miles away, and there was no way for my aunt, my grandmother's oldest child, to get there. Of course, if she had been White, she would have had bus transportation. My grandmother was in a dilemma, wondering where my aunt would attend school after finishing the elementary school. My grandmother finally decided to send my aunt to live with her sister-in-law in Demopolis, Alabama. After completing seventh grade, my aunt was sent to Columbus, Georgia to live with yet another relative so that she could attend school there. My aunt complained about being away from home, but my grandmother explained that it was the only way for her to attain an education.

Years earlier, after my grandmother inherited land, she sold 50 acres and put the money in a savings account. She withdrew the money and purchased a car when my aunt was old enough to drive. This was a wise decision because my mother had now finished the sixth grade and could no longer attend her elementary school. Consequently, my aunt was able to return home to attend Lee County Training School and also drive her younger sister and brother to school.

Most African Americans in the county did not have cars and therefore the family car was always crammed full with other students trying to get to school. In fact, the principal of the school did not have a car, and so my aunt and later my mother drove him around about once a week so that he could conduct school business. The racial climate of the area was such that my grandparents constantly warned their children to slow down when they drove on dirt roads in front of a White person's home, so that they would not stir up too much dust and offend the occupants.

There were 12 students in my mother's graduating senior class. She said most of her elementary classmates dropped out after the sixth grade, with a lack of transportation being a major factor. Some of them did not see the value in getting an education, because there was very little work for an educated African American in a rural area. My uncle said that some African Americans viewed going to school after the sixth grade as a sign of waste and laziness. He stated that those who finished the sixth grade sometimes said, "I got my learning." Friends and relatives criticized my grandmother for taking her savings and purchasing a car, just so her children could go to school.

After my aunt and mother finished high school, my grandfather, concerned with gas costs, decided my uncle should ride a bicycle to school. My grandfather, a World War I veteran, did not value education as my grandmother did and felt that learning farm work was of the utmost importance. In accordance with my grandfather's priorities, my uncle often plowed (with a mule) a field or two before arriving at school by 8:15 a.m.

Although my maternal grandmother left her earthly existence more than 25 years ago, her legacy of respect for education continues to have an impact today. My mother, using her personal funds, established a need-based college scholarship for youth in Anniston, Alabama. My uncle, Charles Harris, Ph.D., who was profiled in the book *A Wealth of Wisdom: Legendary African American Elders Speak* (Cosby

& Poussaint, 2004), donated more than $100,000 to the Political Science Department at Howard University in Washington, DC, to endow a lecture series. He also donated money to establish two scholarships for high school students in Auburn and Opelika, Alabama, and spends an enormous amount of his time helping high school seniors at his church locate and secure college scholarships, often paying their college application fees from his personal funds. Just as with education, a familial habit of reading and respect for its power can also be developed and passed down from one generation to another.

Denial of an education through inaccessibility was a deliberate tactic of some White people who sought to restrict education for African Americans. In Alabama, it was openly discussed that the now Alabama A & M University would be placed in the northern mountains for that purpose. As one Alabama legislator stated, "Since we have to have this institution, I move that we put [William H.] Councill's school up there in the mountains at Huntsville, where it will do the Negroes least good" (Fairclough, 2007, p. 141).

As bad as Alabama was, some places were even worse. Rather than integrate, Prince Edward County in Virginia closed all public schools in the county from 1959 to 1964. The state and county then funneled money and tax credits to private all-White schools while refusing to allocate funds to African American schools, thereby depriving African American students of an education for five years (Virginia Historical Society, n.d.).

During the 1930s, there was no public library open to African Americans where my parents lived. My mother grew up in Auburn, Alabama, home to Auburn University, and there was absolutely no way she could have used the university library. The only library my mother used prior to college was the meager one in her high school that had a few books and one set of encyclopedias.

My parents both said that the only other book in their homes besides their school textbooks was the Bible. My paternal grandparents subscribed to two magazines for farmers, and my maternal grandparents subscribed to one magazine for farmers and a local newspaper. My maternal grandmother sold produce in Auburn, and her White customers were kind enough to give their newspapers to her when they were finished with them. Therefore, my maternal grandfather, an avid reader of newspapers, also had access to newspapers from Montgomery, Birmingham, and Atlanta.

Books were not readily available for my parents, and reading for pleasure was not encouraged by my grandparents, although three of the four grandparents valued education. My grandparents, great-grandparents, and their ancestors had little experience with reading for pleasure as they grew up in the South. One of my three grandparents who valued education was illiterate.

I grew up in Anniston, Alabama, which was relatively progressive by southern standards. For example, in the 1930s and '40s African American schoolchildren were allowed to enter the library once a week on Thursdays and once a month on Sundays. Although the Black community paid taxes to support the public library, their access was limited to these few days a month (Noble, 2003). Later this practice was stopped, probably because at least two small branches for the "colored" became available. One branch was very small. The books were extremely old, and I don't remember seeing anyone in there on the rare occasions that I went there. It was a truly dismal place. At the other branch, children were limited to checking out four books at a time. I assume this limitation existed because of the small number of books for young children on the shelves.

Even with the relative liberalism of White Annistonians, my pastor, a civil rights leader, was severely beaten in the 1960s when he attempted to enter the main branch of the public library where African Americans were no longer allowed. The attack occurred on the same day that 4 African American girls were killed in a church bombing in Birmingham (Noble, 2003). Although he and the other pastor with him survived, the African American community clearly understood the message that was sent. I never set foot in that library.

A few years later, the building that housed that library was closed and demolished. The library was moved to a temporary location. With grave trepidation, I dared to enter. You can imagine my surprise when I discovered that White children had not been limited to checking out only four books at a time. When the new library was constructed on the site of the old, I entered it, still a little apprehensive. Some African Americans remained fearful of entering and did not frequent it at all. Years later, my African American classmate who visited the main library for the first time told me in awe, "Yesterday we went to the White people's library!"

Limiting African Americans' access to libraries was a widespread practice throughout the South. Alice Walker, author of *The Color Purple* (1982), said she was 50 years old before she knew a library even existed in her rural hometown in Georgia. Walker stated that as a result of her upbringing in the South, she is still uncomfortable in libraries and therefore rarely visits them (Walker, 2008).

The African American Past and the Impact on Reading: From Africa to America

My point is that the literacy levels of African Americans should be viewed in a historical context. At least until the 1960s in the South, generations of African Americans grew up without ready access to schools, libraries, books, and/ or reading. My parents, grandparents, great-grandparents, etc., had little or no access to books. My great-great grandparents did not read to my great-grandparents, who did not read to my grandparents, etc. From West Africa to America, conditions did not allow for the development of a familial reading habit to be passed down from generation to generation. A conscious and concerted effort was made to keep African Americans as uneducated as possible. Consequently, "long-term voluntary reading" (Marx, p. B10, 2002) is not widespread throughout our culture, and many may be unaware of its power. We were denied access because of racism, and the effects of decades of denial have manifested in low scores on standardized tests. Now, for those of us with at least access to libraries (Krashen, 2006), we have the power to increase our scores, if we increase our reading.

Chapter 3

Let's Get Technical:
What Are the Scores of African Americans
on Standardized Tests?

In this chapter I present results from various standardized tests. Although African Americans usually make the lowest mean (average) scores, they are not always the lowest. I must emphasize that I am referring to mean scores for the group. You will find that individual African Americans will score much higher on standardized tests than individuals from other ethnic groups. Therefore, please do not assume that every African American received a low score on a standardized test.

The SAT mean was re-centered in 1995, and a revised version of the ACT was implemented in 1989. Therefore, if you are a parent who took the SAT prior to April 1995 or the ACT prior to October 1989, you should not compare your scores to mean scores received after those dates. For the SAT conversion scale, go online (www.collegeboard.com) to find your current score equivalent. For example, if you made an SAT Critical Reading score of 560 in 1972, that would be the 2007 score equivalent of 630. SAT scores range from 200 to 800.

Although when listing SAT mean scores, I use the term "Asian American," the scores of Asians (non U.S. citizens) and Pacific Islanders are also included under this term. I use the term "African American" to report SAT mean scores, but this term also includes the scores of Black examinees who are not American. The scores of Mexicans who are not American citizens are included under the term "Mexican Americans."

The focus of this book is on standardized tests with a major verbal or reading component. For the purpose of informing the reader, I have included some mathematics/ quantitative mean scores.

SAT Reasoning Test: 2007 College-Bound Seniors

Critical Reading – Total Mean Scores by Ethnicity/Group	
Asian, Asian American, or Pacific Islander	578
White	527
Other	497
American Indian or Alaska Native	487
No Response	480
Puerto Rican	459
Other Hispanic, Latino, or Latin American	459
Mexican or Mexican American	455
Black or African American	433
Total Mean	502

Let's Get Technical: What Are the Scores of African Americans on Standardized Tests?

Mathematics	
Asian, Asian American, or Pacific Islander	578
White	534
Other	512
No Response	497
American Indian or Alaska Native	494
Mexican or Mexican American	466
Other Hispanic, Latino, or Latin America	463
Puerto Rican	454
Black or African American	429
Total Mean	515

Writing	
White	518
Asian, Asian American, or Pacific Islander	513
Other	493
No Response	474
American Indian or Alaska Native	474
Mexican or Mexican American	450
Other Hispanic, Latino, or Latin American	450
Puerto Rican	447
Black or African American	425
Total Mean Score	494

Source: www.collegeboard.com. Retrieved August 29, 2007.

African Americans and Standardized Tests

Average Composite Scores on the ACT by Racial and Ethnic Group, 2007	
Asian American	22.6
White	22.1
Other	21.6
American Indian	18.9
Hispanic	18.7
Black	17.0
Total Mean Score	21.2

Source: The Chronicle of Higher Education. (August 31, 2007). Almanac Issue 2007–8. Washington, DC: The Chronicle of Higher Education.

Average ACT Scores in Reading All Ethnicities/Groups	
White	22.5
Asian	22.1
Other/No Response	22.0
American Indian/Alaska Native	19.4
Hispanic	18.8
African American	17.1
Average, All Groups	21.5

Source: ACT (2007). ACT high school profile report: The graduating class of 2007 National, retrieved from the Internet, September 14, 2007, www.act.org/news/data/07/pdf/National2007.pdf.

Let's Get Technical: What Are the Scores of African Americans on Standardized Tests?

Mean GRE General Test Verbal Scores by Ethnic Group: 2004-05	
No Response	522
Other	505
White	497
Asian/Pacific American	493
American Indian	459
Other Hispanic Latin American	447
Mexican American	436
Puerto Rican	409
Black/African American	396
Total Mean Score	484

Mean GRE General Test Quantitative Scores by Ethnic Group: 2004-05	
Asian/Pacific American	627
No Response	592
White	565
Other	560
Other Hispanic Latin American	504
American Indian	500
Mexican American	491
Puerto Rican	476
Black/African American	422
Total Mean Score	550

Source: Factors That Can Influence Performance on the GRE Test 2004–2005 (2007). Princeton, NJ: Educational Testing Service.

African Americans and Standardized Tests

On many tests (e.g., SAT, ACT, GRE), Asian Americans will have the highest mean composite scores (total scores for the entire test). White students often (not always) have the highest mean scores on the verbal or reading section of the tests.

The above test scores indicate that African Americans are scoring the lowest on these standardized tests. Camara and Schmidt (1999) reported that African Americans also had the lowest mean scores on the GMAT and MCAT Physical Sciences and the MCAT Biological Sciences, but not the MCAT Verbal Reasoning, where Hispanics had the lowest mean score.

Another test where African Americans have not consistently scored the lowest is the Law School Admission Test (LSAT). From 1997 to 2004, the mean score of Puerto Ricans was the lowest, with African Americans receiving the next lowest mean scores (Dalessandro, Stilwell, & Reese, 2004). Some contend that law schools, in an effort to increase their rankings, have raised the LSAT score requirements for admission and because African Americans usually score lower than the national average, these higher LSAT score requirements may pose barriers to their admission (MacDonald, 2006; Mangan, 2008; Nussbaumer, 2006).

Let's Get Technical: What Are the Scores of African Americans on Standardized Tests?

LSAT Mean Scores 2003–2004	
No Response	155.37
Caucasian	152.47
Asian American	152.02
Other	150.52
Canadian Aboriginal	150.13
Native American	148.49
Mexican American	147.50
Hispanic	146.52
African American	142.43
Puerto Rican	138.44

Source: Dalessandro, S.P., Stilwell, L.A., & Reese, L.M. (2004). LSAT Performance with regional, gender, and racial/ethnic breakdowns: 1997–1998 through 2003–2004 testing years. Newton, PA: Law School Admission Council, Inc.

There is a relationship between parental income and standardized test scores. As income increases, so do mean test scores (Kobrin, Sathy, & Shaw, 2007). This fact is important because according to a report issued by the U.S. Census Bureau (2007), 24.3% of African Americans live in poverty, compared to 8.2% of Whites, 10.3% of Asians, and 20.6% of Hispanics. The same report stated that African-American households have a median income of $32,000, compared to $64,200, $52,400, and $37,800 for Asian Americans, Whites, and Hispanics, respectively, and that the poverty threshold for a family of four was $20,614 in 2006.

In 2005, 50% of African American children in female headed households lived in poverty, and 13% of African

American children in households with married couples lived in poverty. In White families, however, 33% of children living in female headed households lived in poverty, and only 5% of the children in households with married couples lived in poverty (Federal Interagency Forum on Child and Family Statistics, 2007).

Given the fact that mean test scores usually increase by income, it is understandable that African Americans often have the lowest mean scores. Of the 2007 SAT college-bound seniors, 78% of White examinees and 52% of Asian American seniors came from families making at least $50,000. Only 39% of African American seniors, however, came from families making at least $50,000. Thirty-three percent, 20%, and 10% of White, Asian, and African American college-bound 2007 seniors, respectively, came from families making more than $100,000. As indicated below, a substantial percentage of African American examinees came from families making less than $10,000.

Percentage of Ethnic Group of 2007 SAT College-Bound Seniors from Families Making Less Than $10,000	
African American	11
Other Hispanic	9
Asian	8
Mexican American	8
Puerto Rican	8
Other Ethnic Group	7
American Indian	5
White	1

Source: Derived from data provided by the College Board. Copyright 2007 College Board. www.collegeboard.com.

Let's Get Technical: What Are the Scores of African Americans on Standardized Tests?

Mean Scores for the SAT Critical Reading by Income Subgroups for College-Bound Seniors for 2007	
Less than $10,000	427
$10,000–$20,000	453
$20,000–$30,000	454
$30,000–$40,000	476
$40,000–$50,000	489
$50,000–$60,000	497
$70,000–$80,000	508
$80,000–$100,000	520
More than $100,000	544

Source: Demographic Information. SAT Reasoning Test. New York: College Board. Retrieved from the Internet www.collegeboard.com/cbseniors, September 17, 2007.

It must be noted that the verbal mean score for all 2007 African American college-bound seniors from all income groups (433) is lower than the mean verbal score for all ethnic groups where parental income is between $10,000 and $20,000 (453). Not only are similar results found when you compare SAT Mathematics mean scores (Kobrin, Sathy, Shaw, 2007), Camara and Schmidt (1999) reported that African Americans had mean standardized test scores that were lower than Asian Americans and Whites from comparable income groups.

Now here comes the real shocker: Low-income White students have higher mean scores on almost any (perhaps even every) standardized test than middle-income African Americans, and middle-income White students have higher mean standardized test scores than upper-income African Americans (Camara & Schmidt, 1999). The Mathematics SAT mean scores of Asian Americans from low-income families are higher than African Americans and White students from higher income families (Camara & Schmidt, 1999). The following tables show more recent data.

Asian American 2007 College-Bound Seniors SAT Critical Reading Mean Scores	
Less than $10,000	445
$10,000–$20,000	468
$20,000–$30,000	470
$30,000–$40,000	494
$40,000–$50,000	506
$50,000–$60,000	516
$60,000–$70,000	522
$70,000–$80,000	530
$80,000–$100,000	544
More than $100,000	568

White 2007 College-Bound Seniors SAT Critical Reading Mean Scores	
Less than $10,000	484
$10,000–$20,000	497
$20,000–$30,000	492
$30,000–$40,000	503
$40,000–$50,000	507
$50,000–$60,000	510
$60,000–$70,000	514
$70,000–$80,000	516
$80,000–$100,000	525
More than $100,000	548

LET'S GET TECHNICAL: WHAT ARE THE SCORES OF AFRICAN AMERICANS ON STANDARDIZED TESTS?

Other Ethnic Group 2007 College-Bound Seniors SAT Critical Reading	
Less than $10,000	439
$10,000–$20,000	454
$20,000–$30,000	459
$30,000–$40,000	472
$40,000–$50,000	485
$50,000–$60,000	498
$60,000–$70,000	505
$70,000–$80,000	505
$80,000–$100,000	519
More than $100,000	543

Other Hispanic 2007 College-Bound Seniors SAT Critical Reading	
Less than $10,000	401
$10,000–$20,000	430
$20,000–$30,000	433
$30,000–$40,000	453
$40,000–$50,000	462
$50,000–$60,000	470
$60,000–$70,000	478
$70,000–$80,000	483
$80,000–$100,000	497
More than $100,000	520

American Indian 2007 College-Bound Seniors SAT Critical Reading

Less than $10,000	425
$10,000–$20,000	454
$20,000–$30,000	455
$30,000–$40,000	475
$40,000–$50,000	483
$50,000–$60,000	483
$60,000–$70,000	495
$70,000–$80,000	487
$80,000–$100,000	500
More than $100,000	519

Mexican American 2007 College-Bound Seniors SAT Critical Reading

Less than $10,000	407
$10,000–$20,000	434
$20,000–$30,000	429
$30,000–$40,000	452
$40,000–$50,000	461
$50,000–$60,000	468
$60,000–$70,000	473
$70,000–$80,000	482
$80,000–$100,000	493
More than $100,000	512

Let's Get Technical: What Are the Scores of African Americans on Standardized Tests?

Puerto Rican 2007 College-Bound Seniors SAT Critical Reading	
Less than $10,000	402
$10,000–$20,000	429
$20,000–$30,000	430
$30,000–$40,000	449
$40,000–$50,000	455
$50,000–$60,000	463
$60,000–$70,000	472
$70,000–$80,000	478
$80,000–$100,000	489
More than $100,000	508

African American 2007 College-Bound Seniors SAT Critical Reading	
Less than $10,000	396
$10,000–$20,000	413
$20,000–$30,000	414
$30,000–$40,000	429
$40,000–$50,000	436
$50,000–$60,000	440
$60,000–$70,000	449
$70,000–$80,000	452
$80,000–$100,000	461
More than $100,000	477

Source: Derived from data provided by the College Board. Copyright 2007 College Board. http://www.collegeboard.com.

African Americans and Standardized Tests

African American students from upper-income families have higher mean scores on standardized tests than middle-income African Americans, who have higher mean scores than African American students from low-income families. The same is true of the other ethnic groups as well.

These results reveal, however, that White seniors from families making less than $10,000 a year had a higher mean Critical Reading score (484) than African Americans from families making more than $100,000 (477). This only happened with African Americans. White seniors from families making less than $10,000 did not have higher mean Critical Reading scores than American Indians (519), Mexican Americans (512), etc., who were from families making more than $100,000.

From 1997 to 2007, Asian Americans and American Indians increased their mean Critical Reading scores by 18 and 12 points, respectively, which were the largest gains. Although the 2007 total Critical Reading mean score (514) for Asian Americans as a whole is lower than the total mean score for White seniors (527), Asian Americans from higher income families exceed the mean scores of their White counterparts. Consequently, comparing only by income, Asian Americans at the upper-income levels have the highest Critical Reading mean scores of all ethnic groups.

It is also important to examine the data from the highest level of parental education. Comparing only by parental education, in families where the highest level of parental education is a graduate degree, 2007 college-bound Asian Americans made the highest mean scores in Critical Reading, Mathematics, and Writing.

Let's Get Technical: What Are the Scores of African Americans on Standardized Tests?

Asian American 2007 College-Bound Seniors
SAT Critical Reading Mean Scores
Highest Level of Parental Education

No High School Diploma	446
High School Diploma	474
Associate Degree	488
Bachelor's Degree	517
Graduate Degree	574

White 2007 College-Bound Seniors
SAT Critical Reading Mean Scores
Highest Level of Parental Education

No High School Diploma	457
High School Diploma	487
Associate Degree	498
Bachelor's Degree	535
Graduate Degree	570

Other Ethnic Group 2007 College-Bound Seniors
SAT Critical Reading Mean Scores
Highest Level of Parental Education

No High School Diploma	416
High School Diploma	462
Associate Degree	479
Bachelor's Degree	508
Graduate Degree	547

African Americans and Standardized Tests

American Indian 2007 College-Bound Seniors SAT Critical Reading Mean Scores Highest Level of Parental Education	
No High School Diploma	412
High School Diploma	462
Associate Degree	476
Bachelor's Degree	506
Graduate Degree	533

Mexican American 2007 College-Bound Seniors SAT Critical Reading Mean Scores Highest Level of Parental Education	
No High School Diploma	421
High School Diploma	451
Associate Degree	468
Bachelor's Degree	499
Graduate Degree	515

Other Hispanic 2007 College-Bound Seniors SAT Critical Reading Mean Scores Highest Level of Parental Education	
No High School Diploma	404
High School Diploma	444
Associate Degree	464
Bachelor's Degree	492
Graduate Degree	511

Puerto Rican 2007 College-Bound Seniors SAT Critical Reading Mean Scores Highest Level of Parental Education	
No High School Diploma	404
High School Diploma	441
Associate Degree	454
Bachelor's Degree	480
Graduate Degree	511

African American 2007 College-Bound Seniors SAT Critical Reading Mean Scores Highest Level of Parental Education	
No High School Diploma	391
High School Diploma	414
Associate Degree	430
Bachelor's Degree	453
Graduate Degree	482

Source: Derived from data provided by the College Board. Copyright 2007 College Board. http://www.collegeboard.com.

These scores indicate that White seniors from families where the highest level of parental education is a high school diploma had a higher mean score (487) than that of African Americans from families where the highest level of parental education was a graduate degree (482). This was not true for any other ethnic group. The mean scores of African Americans from families making more than $100,000 or from families where the highest level of parental education is a graduate degree were, however, almost average for the SAT.

I must reiterate that I am referring to mean scores for the group. Not every low-income White student receives a higher SAT score than every middle-class African American child, nor does every middle-class White child outscore every upper-income African American child. In 2001, 1,581 African American students received scores equal to or greater than 1300 (Critical Reading and Mathematics), and 9,195 scored in the 1000 to 1050 range (Bridgeman & Wendler, 2005). Students who score at least 1300 (Critical Reading and Mathematics) and who have good grades in challenging classes are sometimes referred to as "academic superstars" (Bridgeman & Wendler, 2005, p 2). Nevertheless, the fact still remains that the mean scores of lower-income White and Asian American students as a group are higher than the mean scores of African American students from higher income families (as a group), and this is probably a consistent outcome on every standardized test.

For information purposes, I present the Mathematics and Writing mean test scores of 2007 college-bound seniors by income group and highest level of parental education. Although the total mean score of Asian seniors is lower than that of White seniors on the Writing test, as with the Critical Reading test, the mean scores of higher income Asian American students on the Writing test exceed those of their White counterparts. In families where the highest level of parental education is a graduate degree, the mean score of Asian American seniors exceeds that of their White counterparts.

36

Let's Get Technical: What Are the Scores of African Americans on Standardized Tests?

Asian American 2007 College-Bound Seniors SAT Mathematical Mean Scores

Less than $10,000	545
$10,000–$20,000	554
$20,000–$30,000	544
$30,000–$40,000	556
$40,000–$50,000	563
$50,000–$60,000	568
$60,000–$70,000	569
$70,000–$80,000	577
$80,000–$100,000	589
More than $100,000	617

White 2007 College-Bound Seniors SAT Mathematical Mean Scores

Less than $10,000	496
$10,000–$20,000	500
$20,000–$30,000	493
$30,000–$40,000	505
$40,000–$50,000	511
$50,000–$60,000	515
$60,000–$70,000	520
$70,000–$80,000	523
$80,000–$100,000	533
More than $100,000	558

African Americans and Standardized Tests

Other Ethnic Group 2007 College-Bound Seniors SAT Mathematical Mean Scores	
Less than $10,000	476
$10,000–$20,000	480
$20,000–$30,000	474
$30,000–$40,000	482
$40,000–$50,000	494
$50,000–$60,000	505
$60,000–$70,000	510
$70,000–$80,000	514
$80,000–$100,000	526
More than $100,000	555

American Indian 2007 College-Bound Seniors SAT Mathematical Mean Scores	
Less than $10,000	440
$10,000–$20,000	470
$20,000–$30,000	457
$30,000–$40,000	480
$40,000–$50,000	490
$50,000–$60,000	492
$60,000–$70,000	499
$70,000–$80,000	494
$80,000–$100,000	509
More than $100,000	529

Let's Get Technical: What Are the Scores of African Americans on Standardized Tests?

Other Hispanic 2007 College-Bound Seniors SAT Mathematical Mean Scores

Less than $10,000	408
$10,000–$20,000	437
$20,000–$30,000	439
$30,000–$40,000	459
$40,000–$50,000	466
$50,000–$60,000	472
$60,000–$70,000	480
$70,000–$80,000	485
$80,000–$100,000	500
More than $100,000	522

Mexican American 2007 College-Bound Seniors SAT Mathematical Mean Scores

Less than $10,000	420
$10,000–$20,000	449
$20,000–$30,000	446
$30,000–$40,000	465
$40,000–$50,000	472
$50,000–$60,000	477
$60,000–$70,000	480
$70,000–$80,000	490
$80,000–$100,000	497
More than $100,000	518

Puerto Rican 2007 College-Bound Seniors SAT Mathematical Mean Scores

Less than $10,000	399
$10,000–$20,000	426
$20,000–$30,000	424
$30,000–$40,000	443
$40,000–$50,000	447
$50,000–$60,000	460
$60,000–$70,000	466
$70,000–$80,000	473
$80,000–$100,000	485
More than $100,000	506

African American 2007 College-Bound Seniors SAT Mathematical Mean Scores

Less than $10,000	395
$10,000–$20,000	412
$20,000–$30,000	410
$30,000–$40,000	426
$40,000–$50,000	431
$50,000–$60,000	435
$60,000–$70,000	443
$70,000–$80,000	445
$80,000–$100,000	456
More than $100,000	471

Source: Derived from data provided by the College Board. Copyright 2007 College Board. www.collegeboard.com.

Let's Get Technical: What Are the Scores of African Americans on Standardized Tests?

From 1997 to 2007, American Indians and Asian Americans increased their mean scores on the Mathematics test by 19 and 18 points, respectively. White and African American examinees increased their scores by 8 and 6 points, respectively, over the same time period.

The mean Mathematics score (545) of Asian Americans from families making less than $10,000 is a source of inspiration to me. This mean score is higher than the mean scores of White and Other Ethnic Group seniors who come from families making $80,000 to $100,000 and higher than the mean scores of the other groups from families making more than $100,000. I believe they earn these scores because of activities that occur in the home, but that is a discussion for another book. If lower-income Asian American students can achieve in math, then African Americans can achieve as well in reading and in any other area, once we understand how to do it.

Asian American 2007 College-Bound Seniors SAT Mathematics Mean Scores Highest Level of Parental Education	
No High School Diploma	528
High School Diploma	539
Associate Degree	533
Bachelor's Degree	579
Graduate Degree	633

White 2007 College-Bound Seniors
SAT Mathematics Mean Scores
Highest Level of Parental Education

No High School Diploma	465
High School Diploma	495
Associate Degree	507
Bachelor's Degree	543
Graduate Degree	574

Other Ethnic Group 2007 College-Bound Seniors
SAT Critical Mathematics Mean Scores
Highest Level of Parental Education

No High School Diploma	445
High School Diploma	470
Associate Degree	483
Bachelor's Degree	524
Graduate Degree	562

American Indian 2007 College-Bound Seniors
SAT Mathematics Mean Scores
Highest Level of Parental Education

No High School Diploma	435
High School Diploma	468
Associate Degree	485
Bachelor's Degree	513
Graduate Degree	539

Let's Get Technical: What Are the Scores of African Americans on Standardized Tests?

Mexican American 2007 College-Bound Seniors
SAT Mathematics Mean Scores
Highest Level of Parental Education

No High School Diploma	438
High School Diploma	460
Associate Degree	480
Bachelor's Degree	504
Graduate Degree	517

Other Hispanic 2007 College-Bound Seniors
SAT Mathematics Mean Scores
Highest Level of Parental Education

No High School Diploma	414
High School Diploma	448
Associate Degree	465
Bachelor's Degree	494
Graduate Degree	513

Puerto Rican 2007 College-Bound Seniors
SAT Mathematics Mean Scores
Highest Level of Parental Education

No High School Diploma	403
High School Diploma	439
Associate Degree	450
Bachelor's Degree	473
Graduate Degree	499

African American 2007 College-Bound Seniors SAT Mathematics Mean Scores Highest Level of Parental Education	
No High School Diploma	392
High School Diploma	411
Associate Degree	426
Bachelor's Degree	447
Graduate Degree	473

Asian American 2007 College-Bound Seniors SAT Writing Mean Scores	
Less than $10,000	449
$10,000–$20,000	468
$20,000–$30,000	467
$30,000–$40,000	491
$40,000–$50,000	503
$50,000–$60,000	511
$60,000–$70,000	517
$70,000–$80,000	526
$80,000–$100,000	540
More than $100,000	569

Let's Get Technical: What Are the Scores of African Americans on Standardized Tests?

White 2007 College-Bound Seniors SAT Writing Mean Scores	
Less than $10,000	474
$10,000–$20,000	484
$20,000–$30,000	476
$30,000–$40,000	489
$40,000–$50,000	493
$50,000–$60,000	497
$60,000–$70,000	502
$70,000–$80,000	504
$80,000–$100,000	515
More than $100,000	540

Other Ethnic Group 2007 College-Bound Seniors SAT Writing Mean Scores	
Less than $10,000	442
$10,000–$20,000	455
$20,000–$30,000	456
$30,000–$40,000	466
$40,000–$50,000	477
$50,000–$60,000	489
$60,000–$70,000	495
$70,000–$80,000	500
$80,000–$100,000	512
More than $100,000	539

Other Hispanic 2007 College-Bound Seniors SAT Writing Mean Scores

Less than $10,000	395
$10,000–$20,000	423
$20,000–$30,000	424
$30,000–$40,000	444
$40,000–$50,000	453
$50,000–$60,000	459
$60,000–$70,000	469
$70,000–$80,000	474
$80,000–$100,000	487
More than $100,000	511

American Indian 2007 College-Bound Seniors SAT Writing Mean Scores

Less than $10,000	420
$10,000–$20,000	436
$20,000–$30,000	439
$30,000–$40,000	459
$40,000–$50,000	465
$50,000–$60,000	469
$60,000–$70,000	478
$70,000–$80,000	468
$80,000–$100,000	485
More than $100,000	509

Let's Get Technical: What Are the Scores of African Americans on Standardized Tests?

Mexican American 2007 College-Bound Seniors SAT Writing Mean Scores	
Less than $10,000	404
$10,000–$20,000	431
$20,000–$30,000	426
$30,000–$40,000	446
$40,000–$50,000	455
$50,000–$60,000	461
$60,000–$70,000	466
$70,000–$80,000	474
$80,000–$100,000	483
More than $100,000	504

Puerto Rican 2007 College-Bound Seniors SAT Writing Mean Scores	
Less than $10,000	394
$10,000–$20,000	418
$20,000–$30,000	416
$30,000–$40,000	435
$40,000–$50,000	442
$50,000–$60,000	449
$60,000–$70,000	458
$70,000–$80,000	465
$80,000–$100,000	477
More than $100,000	499

African American 2007 College-Bound Seniors
SAT Writing Mean Scores

Less than $10,000	391
$10,000–$20,000	407
$20,000–$30,000	405
$30,000–$40,000	421
$40,000–$50,000	427
$50,000–$60,000	431
$60,000–$70,000	437
$70,000–$80,000	442
$80,000–$100,000	451
More than $100,000	469

Asian American 2007 College-Bound Seniors
SAT Writing Mean Scores
Highest Level of Parental Education

No High School Diploma	442
High School Diploma	472
Associate Degree	482
Bachelor's Degree	517
Graduate Degree	575

Let's Get Technical: What Are the Scores of African Americans on Standardized Tests?

White 2007 College-Bound Seniors SAT Writing Mean Scores Highest Level of Parental Education	
No High School Diploma	448
High School Diploma	477
Associate Degree	486
Bachelor's Degree	525
Graduate Degree	561

Other Ethnic 2007 College-Bound Seniors SAT Writing Mean Scores Highest Level of Parental Education	
No High School Diploma	417
High School Diploma	456
Associate Degree	470
Bachelor's Degree	504
Graduate Degree	544

American Indian 2007 College-Bound Seniors SAT Writing Mean Scores Highest Level of Parental Education	
No High School Diploma	408
High School Diploma	448
Associate Degree	461
Bachelor's Degree	491
Graduate Degree	520

Mexican American 2007 College-Bound Seniors
SAT Writing Mean Scores
Highest Level of Parental Education

No High School Diploma	419
High School Diploma	445
Associate Degree	461
Bachelor's Degree	489
Graduate Degree	505

Other Hispanic 2007 College-Bound Seniors
SAT Writing Mean Scores
Highest Level of Parental Education

No High School Diploma	401
High School Diploma	436
Associate Degree	453
Bachelor's Degree	481
Graduate Degree	500

Puerto Rican 2007 College-Bound Seniors
SAT Writing Mean Scores
Highest Level of Parental Education

No High School Diploma	398
High School Diploma	431
Associate Degree	440
Bachelor's Degree	466
Graduate Degree	498

Let's Get Technical: What Are the Scores of African Americans on Standardized Tests?

African American 2007 College-Bound Seniors SAT Writing Mean Scores Highest Level of Parental Education	
No High School Diploma	385
High School Diploma	406
Associate Degree	420
Bachelor's Degree	443
Graduate Degree	474

Source: Derived from data provided by the College Board. Copyright 2007 College Board. www.collegeboard.com.

I find it interesting that the three percent of 2007 Black examinees who were classified as citizens of other countries had mean SAT scores of 460, 474, and 467 in Critical Reading, Mathematics, and Writing, respectively. These mean scores were higher than the 94 percent of Black examinees who were U.S. citizens or U.S. nationals. Black examinees who were U.S. citizens or nationals had mean scores of 434 (Critical Reading), 429 (Mathematics), and 425 (Writing). The Black examinees who were citizens of other countries did not have the lowest mean scores as compared to other racial/ethnic groups who were citizens of other countries. Without further information, such as parental levels of education, family income, or the countries of their citizenry, I can make note of only the higher mean scores and not draw any other conclusions.

Besides the SAT, another test that reveals the disparity in scores is the National Assessment of Educational Progress (NAEP). The federal government periodically uses

51

standardized tests to determine student progress in certain subject areas. The 2007 NAEP evaluated 350,000 fourth- and eighth-grade students in reading and reported the results (Lee, Grigg, & Donahue, 2007). The achievement levels were Basic (partial mastery of knowledge and skills), Proficient (competency), and Advanced (superior performance). If a fourth-grade student scored at the Advanced level, it meant that he could generalize the information to other topics and could critically evaluate the text. If an eighth-grade student scored at the Advanced level, it meant that he could discuss abstract themes and provide an analysis supported by the text.

The NAEP reported the test results using several factors. For the purpose of this book, I will focus on ethnicity and income. The students were classified according to their eligibility or noneligibility for free or reduced lunch in the National School Lunch Program. The students' eligibility was an indicator of poverty. Below are the average reading scores for the fourth and eighth grades by ethnicity and eligibility for free or reduced lunch.

Grade 4 Reading Average Scores Students Not Eligible for Free or Reduced Lunch	
Asian/ Pacific Islander	239
White	235
American Indian/Alaska Native	219
Latino	217
African American	216

Grade 4 Reading Average Scores Students Eligible for Free or Reduced Lunch	
Asian/ Pacific Islander	217
White	215
Latino	199
African American	198
American Indian/Alaska Native	195

Percent at Advanced Achievement Level for Grade 4 Reading	
Asian/ Pacific Islander	15
White	11
American Indian/Alaska Native	4
Latino	3
African American	2

Asian/Pacific Islanders had the highest mean scores. African Americans did not have the lowest mean score in the eligible classification, although they did in the not-eligible classification. What is important about these results, however, is that Asian/Pacific Islanders from the eligible classification (indicating some degree of poverty in the family) had a higher mean score than African Americans from families with incomes that made them ineligible for free or reduced lunch. White students from the eligible classification had a mean score almost equal to African American students who were not eligible.

Fortunately, there is good news. Since 1992, African Americans as a group have increased their scores by 11 points. Asian Americans/Pacific Islanders, Latino, and White students have increased their scores by 16, 8, and 6 points, respectively.

Grade 8 Reading Average Scores Students Not Eligible for Free or Reduced Lunch	
Asian/ Pacific Islander	278
White	275
American Indian/Alaska Native	259
Latino	257
African American	254

Grade 8 Reading Average Scores Students Eligible for Free or Reduced Lunch	
White	258
Asian/Pacific Islander	257
Latino	242
American Indian/Alaska Native	240
African American	239

Let's Get Technical: What Are the Scores of African Americans on Standardized Tests?

Percent at Advanced Achievement Level for Grade 8 Reading	
Asian/ Pacific Islander	5
White	4
American Indian/Alaska Native	2
Latino	1
African American	.42 (rounds to 0)

Again, Asian Americans/Pacific Islanders had the highest mean score. Both Asian/Pacific Islander and White eighth-grade students who were eligible for free or reduced lunch had higher mean scores (257 and 258, respectively) than African American students (254) who were not eligible for free or reduced lunch.

Why do these score differences between lower income White and Asian American students and higher income African Americans occur? I maintain that the answer lies in the amount of reading done by these ethnic groups. I will provide evidence of this assertion in Chapter 4 in the "African Americans and Reading" section.

In spite of the high scores of Asian American students on various standardized tests, some claim that aggregate reporting of scores for all Asian groups hides the fact that some Asian ethnic groups are not performing well academically (Redondo, Aung, Fung, & Yu, 2008). These Asian students, who defy the model minority stereotype, are in need of bilingual programs, assessments in their native language, and other services that school districts rarely provide. Advocates recommend that No Child Left Behind distinguish between the different Asian ethnicities so as to identify struggling students who often fail and/or leave school. Indeed, just looking at standardized test scores may not provide an accurate academic picture of any racial or ethnic group.

Chapter 4

What Causes These Score Differences?

Researchers have suggested various causes for the differences in scores. Wiesen (2006) reviewed the literature and listed more than 100 possible causes. He grouped them into several categories based on whether the causes were inherited or not inherited. The list of possible inherited causes was quite brief. One inherited cause, sickle cell anemia, was listed because of its effect on school attendance. Most of the causes, which were not inherited, included the perceived oral tradition (less reading) of African American culture and not enough time spent reading aloud to young children. Wiesen stated that all the reasons he compiled together could possibly account for much of the differences in mean scores, whereas one reason alone would possibly account for only a small amount of the difference.

In reviewing the research literature, Ferguson (2005) found that teacher quality, the impact of the teacher's race, preschools, and class size have been studied to determine their roles in enhancing academic achievement. He stated that all these factors can play a role in increasing student achievement. There is also research linking teacher absenteeism to low student achievement. One study found that teacher absences had a negative effect on annual state math test scores and a smaller effect on language arts test scores (Miller, Murname, & Willett, 2007, as cited in Keller, 2008).

Some research has even examined the lyrics of hip-hop/rap music to determine its impact on academic achievement and education (Gosa, 2007). The messages in rap music were analyzed because substantial numbers of young African Americans listen to rap music.

Scientists have reviewed the literature regarding the effects of poverty and stress on the brain (National Scientific Council on the Developing Child, 2007). They concluded that brains are "built over time" (p. 1) and poverty and conditions associated with poverty can negatively affect brain development in infants.

Some have suggested that enrolling low-income students into middle-class schools is another way to boost academic achievement (Glater & Finder, 2007). Wake County, North Carolina, which includes Raleigh, has had success with raising the achievement scores of African Americans and Latinos by enrolling them into middle-class schools. Busing and school assignments were used to limit the percentage of low-income students to no more than 40% per school (Finder, 2006). In 2006, 82% of African Americans in Wake County scored at grade level on state reading tests, an increase from only 40% in 1995 (Glater & Finder, 2007).

The socioeconomic status of the school population may be significant inasmuch as many public schools are primarily low-income. Most public school students in the South are from low-income families, and public schools in the West will probably indicate similar levels of poverty in 5 to 7 years (Abdullah, 2007). One-third or more of school populations in Milwaukee, Cleveland, Detroit, St. Louis, and Fresno, California, are already living in poverty (Glauber & Poston, 2008).

As discussed in the previous chapter, middle-income African Americans score lower on standardized tests than their White counterparts. Gosa and Alexander (2007) reviewed the literature regarding this issue and concluded that although these groups might on the surface appear to be similar, certain differences existed. The peer group of African American students may not support academic achievement. African American families lack family wealth, are relatively new arrivals to the middle-class, and have less income. Differences in parenting styles between White and African American parents may occur because African American parents may feel the need to prepare their children to deal with racism. African American parents may not be as assertive in their interactions with school personnel as White parents, and they may also have to expend resources to deal with racism in areas such as housing, employment, salary, and purchasing.

Gosa and Alexander (2007) also discussed differences among racial and ethnic groups as relevant to education. Segregated schools, segregation within schools due to tracking and therefore preventing enrollment in advanced courses, and African American students' poor interpersonal relationships with teachers may also contribute to the achievement gap.

Instead of focusing on the achievement gap, some researchers studied minority students who excelled on the SAT (Bridgeman & Wendler, 2005). The researchers stated that regardless of ethnicity, students who achieved in challenging classes also had high SAT scores. They weren't sure whether "succeeding in demanding courses leads to high SAT scores, or whether possessing the reading and math skills measured by the SAT causes students to do well in these courses" (p. 2) They advocated a multipronged approach for decreasing the achievement gap that would include enrolling students in challenging classes, developing students' reading and math skills, and considering other factors that could affect test performance (e.g., teacher competency).

African Americans and Standardized Tests

The theory of "stereotype threat" has also received quite a bit of attention in academia. In the context of testing, stereotype threat may occur when a student believes he may confirm, through his performance on a test, an existing negative perception of the group to which he belongs. This belief can detrimentally affect his performance on the test (Steele, 2004; Frontline, n.d.). Stereotype threat is also being studied in other contexts, such as interracial interactions (Goff, Steele, & Davies, 2008).

I do not denigrate other researchers' theories regarding the reasons for these score differences, with the exception of one. I wholeheartedly denounce any theory that espouses the idea that score differences occur because of innate intellectual deficits with African Americans as a group of people. I refer you to the work of Fryer and Levitt (2006), Nisbett (1998), Gould (1996), and Lewontin, Rose, and Kamin (1984) to explain in part why I denounce such theories. Otherwise, I believe all theories should be thoroughly investigated. The research findings should be considered and possibly applied to improve the academic achievement of African American students.

It is my belief, however, that these score differences occur because of a lack of long-term reading, beginning at birth (i.e., parents not reading to their infants). Also, solutions for some of the other proposed causes rely on a dependence on others, be it teachers or politicians, to remedy the situation. I prefer to examine what people/parents can do for themselves.

Please note that whenever I advocate that children read more, I am of course also advocating for the successful comprehension of what is read (Topping, Samuels, & Paul, 2007). Later in the book, I provide suggestions for parents that will help them promote comprehension.

What Causes These Score Differences?

The Importance of Reading

Fischgrund (2004) conducted research that is relevant to this book. He studied 160 out of 541 students who made perfect scores on the SAT in 2000. The students completed questionnaires, and Fischgrund also interviewed some of them. At the time of his study, a perfect score was 1600. (Currently, with the recently added Writing Section, a perfect score is 2400.) He also compared them to a group of test takers (the "control group") that scored from 1000 to 1200 in Critical Reading and Mathematics, which he said were average to slightly above average scores. It is important to keep in mind that for 2005 college bound seniors, when the score of 1000 based on 2 parts represented average, African American seniors averaged 864, 136 points below the average score of 1000. For 2007 college bound seniors, only upper income African Americans and those from well-educated families had mean scores slightly below average.

Based on his research, Fischgrund listed the seven secrets of those perfect score students. Reading, of course, was one of the seven secrets. In fact, Fischgrund described it as being "crucial" to success (p. 92). The perfect score students' number one test-taking tip was to "read everything" (p. 187).

What is particularly interesting is what Fischgrund found about the amount of time perfect score students spent reading versus the control group. Perfect score students spent an average of 9 hours a week reading for school and 5 hours a week reading for pleasure (not connected with school assignments) for a total of 14 hours per week. The control group averaged 4 hours a week reading for school assignments and 4 hours a week reading for pleasure for a total of 8 hours per week.

Therefore, the question for African Americans parents is, "How much time does your child spend reading each week? Does your child spend about 4 hours reading for pleasure each week?" Remember, for 2007 college bound African Americans seniors, the mean score was 1287, 213 points below the test midpoint of 1500. On the Critical Reading section, the African American mean for 2007 seniors was 433, 67 points lower than the designated test midpoint of 500. Therefore, approximately 8 hours of reading per week (4 for school assignments, 4 for pleasure) may be necessary, just to get the African American average (as a group) closer to the 1000 (two parts) or 1500 (three parts) mean.

The issue of how much homework or amount of time spent reading for homework may also be a factor. Some educators have concluded from the research that the relationship between homework and academic achievement is stronger for older students but less evident for younger students (Cooper & Valentine, 2001). It has been suggested that students in kindergarten through the second grade should have 10 to 20 minutes of homework per day. For students in the third through sixth grades, the guideline is for 30 to 60 minutes per day and then for the seventh through twelfth grades, homework will vary depending on the subject (Henderson, 1996).

Other characteristics about the perfect score students concerned their schools and family composition. Fischgrund found that 80% of the students attended public schools and 90% were from intact families.

There are others who contend that more reading equals better readers (Schatmeyer, 2007; Gambrell, 2007) and that parents should read to their infants every day (Honig, 2007). Librarians have created programs designed to get parents to enroll their infants and toddlers in summer reading programs for the purpose of developing literacy skills (Arnold & Colburn, 2007).

The National Assessment of Educational Progress (NAEP) scores and differences between African Americans and other ethnic groups were listed in the previous chapter. According to the Educational Testing Service (Barton & Coley, 2007), four factors can predict the average scores of entire states on the NAEP eighth-grade reading test: 1) the percentage of children in single parent households, 2) student absences, 3) hours spent watching television, and 4) children from birth through age 5 who are read to every day. When researchers used these factors to predict state scores, they came very close to the actual scores. They referred to the family as America's smallest school.

Reading to infants is so important that one researcher, Robert Titzer, founded a company that markets "Your Baby Can Read" DVDs and other products (Your Baby Can Read, n.d.). Titzer believes that children's educational development is dependent on teaching infants to read as early as possible. On his Web site (www.yourbabycanread.com), you'll see a video of an infant responding correctly to words printed on flashcards. For example, the word "hand" is shown, and the infant looks at the printed word and waves her hand. Titzer also discusses research studies regarding the benefits of early reading on his Web site. He has appeared on several national television shows discussing his theories.

Although I am not endorsing Titzer's products, if I had an infant, I would probably purchase them. I would still, however, begin reading to my child on the day he was born and continue to read at least one story to him each day.

African Americans and Standardized Tests

There is also research focused on older children. Researchers asked 155 fifth graders to record how they spent their time outside of school during a time period that varied from 2 to 6 months (Anderson, Wilson, & Fielding, 1986). The forms were created after discussions with the subjects about how they spent their time outside school. The activities included, but were not limited to, listening to music, playing sports, doing chores, and reading. If they read a book, they were asked to give the name and author of the book.

Three reading tests were administered which assessed reading comprehension, vocabulary, and reading speed. The researchers also reviewed test results from the students' files from the second grade. Based on interviews with some of the children and their parents, the researchers found that children who read often in the fifth grade had begun this habit in the third or fourth grade. The researchers concluded that teachers played a major role in influencing the amount of time students spent reading books and that the time spent reading books was the best predictor of reading progress.

Other studies have found evidence of practice affecting reading achievement. Topping, Samuels, & Paul (2007) studied the reading records of 45,670 students who used Accelerated Reader. With Accelerated Reader, students read a book and then take a quiz about the book on the computer. Accelerated Reader records the percentage of questions answered correctly on each quiz. The researchers analyzed the data from Accelerated Reader as well as the students' standardized test scores in reading. They concluded that both quality (indicated by reading comprehension) and quantity of reading were necessary for high achievement gains in reading.

Bus, Van IJzendoorn, and Pellegrini (1995) reviewed several studies regarding joint book reading (i.e., parents reading to their children). They found that when parents read to their preschool children, the reading had an effect on achievement and language development. The researchers stated that as written language is more complex than spoken language, it is important to read to children at a young age to familiarize them with the structure of written language.

Researchers have examined the effects of joint book reading. For example, Ard and Beverly (2004) studied the effect of joint book reading on learning nonsense words. Nonsense words, as the term implies, are not real words. One reason the researchers created nonsense words was to preclude the possibility that the children could have learned the words in another setting. Their study sample consisted of 40 children between 36 and 59 months of age with normal language development. The children were divided into four groups: 1) joint book reading only, 2) joint book reading and asking the child questions, 3) joint book reading and making comments to the child, and 4) joint book reading with questions and comments. The questions and comments were scripted. While all methods were beneficial for learning words, joint book reading with questions and comments was more beneficial than joint book reading alone. The joint book reading with questions and comments and the joint book reading with comments groups named more new words than the joint book reading only or joint book reading with questions groups.

Researchers have also studied emergent literacy. Emergent literacy refers to the skills a child uses to learn about words, reading, and/or writing prior to formal instruction (The Online Teacher Resource, n.d.). For example, children have a basic understanding that written words transmit meaning or they may have a basic knowledge of letter names (Literacy Guide, n.d.)

African Americans and Standardized Tests

In one study, researchers investigated whether training mothers on how to comment during joint book reading sessions would improve the children's emergent literacy (Hockenberger, Goldstein, & Haas, 1999). Seven low-income families with children ranging from 53 to 63 months participated in the study. Four of the mothers were African American and 3 were White. The mothers were high school graduates and had at least an eighth-grade reading level. The researchers administered a battery of tests to the children and determined that 3 of the children had developmental disabilities. The mothers received training for 3 hours a week for 8 weeks. The mothers read to the children and taped the sessions. The audiotapes were returned to the researchers. The children were assessed before and after the intervention. The researchers found that the training increased the mothers' comments and improved the children's emergent literacy. Four of the mothers indicated that they would continue reading to their children.

Eppe Chamberlain (2003) studied emergent literacy in 214 African American and 102 Latino preschoolers. One hundred thirty-four boys and 182 girls ranging in age from 32 to 62 months (with 47 months being the mean age) participated in the study. Chamberlain looked at maternal leisure reading, reading exposure, participation in library reading programs, reading engagement, book ownership, and print exposure. Reading exposure comprised activities such as the mother reading to the child and the child going to the library. Print exposure included a mother teaching her child the alphabet or the child attempting to write words. Reading engagement examined behaviors such as whether the child lost interest during the reading period and whether more than one book was read.

What Causes These Score Differences?

The Peabody Picture Vocabulary Test-Revised (PPVT-R) was used to assess the children's receptive vocabulary. The mothers completed two questionnaires. The Latino children had higher scores on the PPVT-R. The Latino mothers reported more maternal leisure reading, higher reading exposure for the children, greater participation in library reading programs, and more child's reading engagement. On the survey, the Latino mothers indicated stronger agreement "with positive beliefs about reading" (p. 20). African American mothers reported greater book ownership, greater exposure to print for their children, and they also reported that they began to read to their children earlier than Latino mothers. The two activities that predicted oral language scores were reading exposure and reading engagement. This finding is important because other studies have indicated that oral language is related to reading ability.

Raikes, et al. (2006) collaborated with other researchers to study the effects of joint book reading in 2,581 low-income mothers. Thirty-seven percent of the mothers were White, 34% African American, 17% Spanish-speaking Latino, 6% English-speaking Latino, and 4% were members of other ethnic groups. The researchers examined several factors including but not limited to the percent of mothers reading to their children, the access to books, the characteristics of the mothers, and the effect of joint book reading. They asked the mothers to report their book reading frequency when the children were 14, 24, and 36 months of age.

Of the total sample of mothers, 48.3 percent of the mothers read daily when their children were 14 months of age. At 14 months of age, 77.6 percent of African American children had at least five books in the home compared to 90.7 percent of White mothers. When the children were 24 and 36

67

months of age, African American mothers were less likely to report reading daily to their children than White mothers. At 36 months of age, the children were administered the Peabody Picture Vocabulary Test III. On the basis of the study, the researchers concluded that daily reading predicted children's language skills. They also asserted that it was important for book reading to begin before age three.

Another researcher examined the effects of reading for pleasure on African American students (Flowers, 2003). She reviewed data from the National Education Longitudinal Study. A conclusion of the study was that reading for pleasure (reading not required for school) seemed to have a positive effect on African American students' performance on a standardized reading test. The researcher recommended that teachers encourage and design activities to promote leisure (pleasure) reading.

The National Endowment for the Arts (2007) issued a report on literacy that was based on data collected by various federal governmental agencies. The review indicated that students who read more perform better on reading and writing tests. Among twelfth-grade students (2005–2006), as the number of books in the home increased, so did scores on standardized tests in science, civics, and history. Students from homes that had more than 100 books had the highest mean scores on these tests and those with zero to ten books in the home had the lowest mean scores.

The report also showed value in reading aside from its effect on standardized test scores. Better readers earn more money. Readers are more likely to be engaged in society by voting, participating in charity work, and attending plays and sporting events. They are more likely to visit museums, create art, and exercise. In other words, reading can help your child become a well-rounded, productive citizen. Cunningham and Stanovich (1998) concluded that reading increases vocabulary more than oral language, and it makes a child smarter.

Alexander, Entwisle, & Olson (2007) studied data from the Beginning School Study panel, a project that targeted students in the Baltimore City Public School System. They concluded that much of the reading achievement gap between lower- and upper-income students could be attributed to how time was spent during the summer in the elementary school years. Students in this project were randomly selected in the first grade and were followed until age 22. The researchers examined the students' files, reviewed interviews with students, and obtained data from the parents' questionnaires. They stated that most of the achievement up through the ninth grade was a result of the impact of school. They also stated that low scores on standardized tests can play a role in preventing low-income students from being placed into college preparatory courses.

The term "summer slide" is sometimes used to explain what happens to reading achievement during summer vacation (Cech, 2007). Research has indicated that during the summer, low-income students do not read as much as upper-income students. It has also been referred to as the "Harry Potter Divide" meaning that low-income children did not read the popular series, or do other reading. (Krueger, 2000). The question for all African American parents is, "How much does your child read during the summer?"

Some programs have been developed to mitigate the summer slide. African American and Latino students at Harvard Law founded Building Educated Leaders for Life (BELL), which offers year-round and summer academic programs. During the summer, students receive 8 hours of literacy instruction per week. Chaplin and Capizzano (2006) compared students in the BELL program to a control group that did not participate in the program. BELL students read more books in the time period than the control group and improved their reading test scores more than the students in the control group.

Computers and the Internet are an integral part of everyday life for many in American society. Therefore, it is no surprise that the relationship between the Internet and academic performance has been studied. Researchers studied home Internet access and academic achievement in children who were from low-income families and who were performing below average in school (Jackson, et al., 2006). The study subjects consisted of 140 children, of whom 83% were African American and 58% male. Seventy-five percent of the children lived in single-parent households. They ranged in age from 10 to 18, with the average age being 13.8. The median family income was $15,000. Prior to the study, the families had not had home Internet access. The families received computers, technical support, and Internet access as part of the study. The parents agreed to have their Internet use automatically recorded for 16 months. The children's GPAs and scores on the Michigan Educational Assessment Program standardized tests in reading and math were obtained at several different times during and/or after the study.

The computers were used mainly for school assignments, with the students visiting Web pages that contained primarily text. The students seldom used the computers for communication. The researchers speculated that this was because their extended family members and friends did not have home Internet access. Many of the parents prohibited their children from participating in online activities that would put them in contact with strangers.

What Causes These Score Differences?

During the study, African American and younger children used the Internet less than White children and older children. The researchers noted that the students were reading more and that more Internet use was associated with higher standardized reading test scores, but there was no effect on standardized math scores. The researchers also stated, however, that these participants were well below average academically and that perhaps the same results would not occur for students who were already exhibiting at least average academic performance.

Although the results of this study are promising, at least as it concerns reading and reading achievement, the federal government released a report regarding the racial and socioeconomic digital divide that existed as late as 2003 (Debell & Chapman, 2006). The report stated that children from well-educated parents were more likely to use computers and the Internet. According to the authors, 58% of Asian American children, 54% of White children, 47% of American Indians, and 27% of African American children used the Internet at home. Fortunately, they found the digital divide less evident at school.

The city of Birmingham, Alabama, is attempting to lessen the impact of the digital divide. In 2008, the city council approved plans to purchase 1,000 computers from the One Laptop Per Child nonprofit organization as part of a pilot program to study the impact of giving computers to children. The goal is to give each child in the first through eighth grades an inexpensive computer (Birmingham approves low-cost laptop project, 2008).

The emphasis on reading is not just an American phenomenon (Hall, 2001). Throughout the world, educators and librarians have created literacy programs to promote early reading experiences for young children. In Australia, a program called Better Beginnings was developed and focused on children from birth to 3 years of age. The program helped parents develop the skills necessary to read to their infants and toddlers (North & Allen, 2005).

Although the focus of this book is on reading, reading can also affect mathematics performance, and some studies have looked at the relationship between reading and mathematics. Clements and Sarama (2006) reviewed the research literature and stated that there is a connection between math and literacy skills. They also listed books for young children that have math-related aspects in the storylines. Others have indicated that the reading problems of children may detrimentally affect their math achievement (Gersten, Jordan, & Flojo, 2005). O'Neill, Pearce, and Pick (as cited in O'Neill, 2004) found that children who scored high on a storytelling task when they were 3 and 4 years old also scored higher on a math achievement test two years later.

African Americans and Reading

There is evidence that some African Americans do not read to their children on a daily basis, beginning when their children are infants. According to the federal government, 68% of White children are read to every day, compared to 50% of African American children. The report also stated that children living with one parent are less likely to be read to than children living with two parents. This is a significant finding because in 2006, 35% of African American children lived with two married parents contrasted with 76% of White children. Children from families at or above the poverty line are more likely to be read to every day than children from families below the poverty line (Federal Interagency Forum on Child and Family Statistics, 2007). As stated in Chapter 3,

What Causes These Score Differences?

24.3% of African Americans live in poverty (U.S. Census Bureau, 2007), and 50% of African American children in female-headed households lived in poverty in 2005 (Federal Interagency Forum on Child and Family Statistics, 2007).

As noted in a previously mentioned study, low-income African American mothers were less likely to read daily to their children than were low- income White mothers (Raikes, et al., 2006), and this was not the only study to state this conclusion. Other studies have found similar results.

Yarosz and Barnett (2001) studied the frequency of parents reading to their children. The researchers analyzed data from the National Household Education Survey of 1995. The data were collected via telephone interviews with the parents and guardians of 7,566 children under the age of 6. The average age of the children was 2.1. The sample of children comprised 60.9% White, 13.5% African American, 20% Latino, and 5.6% were classified as other. The category of "other" consisted of Asian, Pacific Islanders, and Native Americans.

Regardless of their educational attainment, African American parents read less frequently to their children than White parents. Forty-seven percent of White families where the mother had less than a high school education, reported that their children were read to every day, which was the same percentage for African American families where the mothers had at least a college degree. In contrast, 69% of White families where the mother had at least a college degree reported reading to their children every day. In White families where the mother had at least a high school diploma, a greater percentage (56%) reported reading daily to their children than their African American counterparts (38%) and African American families where the mother had at least a college degree (47%).

African Americans and Standardized Tests

In English-speaking Latino families where the mothers had at least a college degree, 66% reported reading to their children every day. Only 47% of their African American counterparts reported the same. This may partially explain why on the SAT the various Latino groups increase in Critical Reading mean scores as income and education level increases (see Chapter 3) such that the students from Latino families earning over $100,000 or students from well-educated families average above 500. Thirty-two percent of Latino families where the mothers had less than a high school diploma and 45% where mothers had at least a high school diploma reported reading daily to their children. For Latinos whose primary language was not English, the percentages that reported reading daily were much less. Fourteen percent, 29%, and 28% of families where the mothers had less than a high school diploma, at least a high school diploma, and at least a college degree, respectively, reported reading daily.

On the other hand, African American families where the mothers had at least a college degree had the lowest percentage of mothers (4%) who reported that they never read to their children. This figure is encouraging. Five percent, 9%, and 30% of their White, English-speaking Latino, and non-English-speaking Latino counterparts, respectively, reported the same.

There is another study that is particularly relevant to the assertions in this book. In this study, researchers investigated the home environments of American children (Bradley, Corwyn, McAdoo, & Coll, 2001). They analyzed data from the National Longitudinal Survey of Youth (NLSY). The NLSY collected data through home observations and interviews. The results they reported may also help explain why low-income White students usually have higher mean scores on standardized tests than middle-income African

What Causes These Score Differences?

Americans and why middle-income White students have higher mean scores than upper-income African Americans. Although they reported the data from several different aspects, I will focus on ethnicity and income. The researchers used the terms "poor" and "nonpoor" to refer to the socioeconomic status of the families.

Children's Ages:
Birth to 2 years, 11 months

Percentage Reporting Reading At Least 3 Times a Week to Daily	
White	66.7 of nonpoor mothers
	44.9 of poor mothers
African American	43.8 of nonpoor mothers
	31.7 of poor mothers

Percentage Reporting 10 or More Books in the Home	
White	63 of nonpoor mothers
	41.8 of poor mothers
African American	33 of nonpoor mothers
	19.7 of poor mothers

African Americans and Standardized Tests

The percentage of nonpoor African Americans reading at least three times a week was almost equal to the percentage of poor Whites but not equal to the percentage of nonpoor Whites. The NLSY also questioned mothers about the number of books in the home. A greater percentage of poor White mothers (41.8%) reported having 10 or more books in the home than nonpoor African American mothers (33%).

For 3 to 5 years, 11 months

Percentage Reporting Reading At Least 3 Times a Week to Daily	
White	71.4 of nonpoor mothers
	55.4 of poor mothers
African American	45 of nonpoor mothers
	33.3 of poor mothers

Percentage Reporting 10 or More Books in the Home	
White	93.4 of nonpoor mothers
	74.6 of poor mothers
African American	67.8 of nonpoor mothers
	39.9 of poor mothers

What Causes These Score Differences?

Again, more poor White mothers reported reading to their children at least three times a week than nonpoor African American mothers. The White nonpoor mothers also reported reading to their children more than their African American counterparts. A greater percentage of poor White mothers reported having 10 or more books in the home than African American mothers who were not poor.

6 to 9 years, 11 months

Percentage Reporting Reading At Least 3 Times a Week to Daily	
White	45.2 of nonpoor mothers
	35.7 of poor mothers
African American	30.3 nonpoor mothers
	28.0 of poor mothers

Percentage Reporting 10 or More Books in the Home	
White	94.7 of nonpoor mothers
	80.3 of poor mothers
African American	75.3 of nonpoor mothers
	47.8 of poor mothers

African Americans and Standardized Tests

10 to 14 years, 11 months

Percentage Reporting 10 or More Books in the Home	
White	73.5 of nonpoor mothers
	50.9 of poor mothers
African American	41.6 of nonpoor mothers
	26.1 of poor mothers

Regarding children 10 to 14 years old, a greater percentage of African American mothers who were not poor had 10 or more books in the home than poor African American mothers. A greater percentage of poor White mothers, however, reported that they had 10 or more books than nonpoor African American mothers.

The researchers also found that the percentage of Asian American families reading at least three times a week or more to their children increased over time. Although White families were more likely to read to their children, "the dramatic increase among Asian Americans closed the gap by the time children went to school" (p. 1860). The researchers did not divide the Asian American subjects into poor and nonpoor categories because they did not have enough poor Asian American mothers in the study.

Ferguson (2005) surveyed advantaged and disadvantaged elementary African American, Asian, Latino, and White students from mainly suburban school districts. Advantaged students were defined as those with at least two adults and a computer in the home. Disadvantaged students were defined as those who had a single parent and/or did not have a computer at home.

Ferguson found that the percentage of advantaged African American children who reported reading every day at home was not only less than advantaged students from the other ethnic groups, it was less than the number of disadvantaged students from the other ethnic groups as well. The number of disadvantaged African Americans who reported reading every day was the lowest of all the groups and socioeconomic classifications.

A greater percentage (83%) of disadvantaged African Americans reported having a television in their bedrooms than all advantaged (including African Americans) and disadvantaged groups. Eighty-one percent of advantaged African Americans reported having a television in their bedrooms, which was the second highest percentage. Thirty percent of advantaged African Americans reported that they watched television at home more than they did anything else. This was a greater percentage than the advantaged and disadvantaged students of the other ethnic groups. Thirty-six percent of the disadvantaged African Americans reported that they watched more television at home than they did anything else. A far greater percentage of African Americans, advantaged and disadvantaged, reported watching rap videos than the other ethnic groups, advantaged and disadvantaged.

These studies help explain why low-income White students have higher mean scores than middle-income African Americans. From birth, low-income White students may have more experience with the main skill (reading) of tests with a verbal focus than African Americans from higher income groups. White students from middle-income families may have more experience with reading than their middle-income African American counterparts, low-income White students, and low-income African American students. Low-income African American students have the least amount of experience with reading starting from birth and as a result, have the lowest mean scores. The lack of African American children's experiences with books has been noted previously (Washington, 2001).

A poll taken of 508 adolescents, ages 12 to 18, presents a different perspective (Teen book club, 2001). Seventy-five percent of these students reported that they were "good students," whereas 16% reported that they were average. Only 8% reported that they were "not that good a student." More African American and Latino students said their parents encouraged reading than White students, and more African American and Latino students reported reading to others at least a few times a week than the White respondents. Fifty percent of African Americans, 40% of Latinos, and 37% of White teens indicated they read more than 15 books in the previous year. On a scale of 1 to 5 with 5 being the most enjoyment from reading, 56% of Latinos, 51% of African Americans, and 47% of White students rated the enjoyment they got from reading as 4 or 5.

Unfortunately, based on the information that I could find about the poll, there were no data that indicated how these students performed on standardized test scores or whether the students were read to as infants. Nevertheless, the results should encourage parents and teachers. If African American children can be convinced of the importance of reading, they may begin to turn off the television and pick up a book.

Chapter 5

Literacy and the Criminal Justice System

Researchers have examined the implications of reading for social adjustment and juvenile delinquency. Benner, Beaudoin, Kinder, and Mooney (2005) studied beginning reading skills and their relationship to social adjustment. Their sample consisted of 150 children in kindergarten through second grade. Tests were administered to the children to measure their literacy skills and auditory comprehension. Their teachers completed the Social Skills Rating System to assess the social adjustment of the children. They found that beginning reading skills were related to social and academic skills.

Researchers have studied whether academic programs can increase literacy skills. Drakeford (2002) studied 6 African American males in a correctional facility with low reading achievement as measured by the Wide Range Achievement Test and the Corrective Reading Placement Test. The average age of the subjects was 17. The juveniles received decoding and comprehension instruction for 3 hours a week for 8 weeks and were evaluated after each lesson. The Rhody-Secondary Reading Attitude Assessment was used to determine reading attitude. As a result of the program, all juveniles improved in reading fluency and reading grade level. They also showed improvements in their attitudes toward reading.

Mann and Reynolds (2006) studied data from the Chicago Longitudinal Study (CLS). They looked at the records of 1,406 youth who had received education prior to the first grade (preschool). The researchers studied the incidence, severity, and frequency of juvenile delinquency, among other

81

outcome measures. They found that a preschool education was related to decreased juvenile delinquency.

Archwamety and Katsiyannis (2000) reviewed the files of 505 delinquent males, ages 12 to 18, who lived in a correctional facility. They compared students who had received remediation in either math or reading to juveniles in the facility who had not received remediation. Students in a remedial group were at least one grade level behind in reading or math and below the 50th percentile. They concluded that academic achievement is a factor in delinquency and recidivism. They stated that early remediation might prevent youth from entering the criminal justice system.

McMackin, Tansi, and Hartwell (2005) examined the records of 144 juvenile offenders in a residential treatment center in order to reach some conclusions about basic academic skills and escape risk. Those with at least a ninth-grade level of vocabulary skills and reading comprehension were more likely to graduate from the program while those with less than a sixth-grade skills level were more likely to attempt an escape. Those with math skills at or above the ninth-grade level had the lowest recidivism rate. Vocabulary skills and reading comprehension had no relationship to recidivism.

The literacy levels of inmates have also been studied. On behalf of the U.S. Department of Education, Greenberg, Dunleavy, and Kutner (2007) studied the literacy levels of 1,200 inmates in state and federal prisons. The inmates were at least 16 years of age and were representative of the 1,380,000 prison inmates in 2003. Ninety-four percent of the inmate population was male, and 6% female.

The inmates were asked to complete tasks involving literacy. The same tasks were administered to 18,000 adults in households (hereinafter referred to as "household adults") who were not incarcerated. The assessment examined prose, document, and quantitative literacy. The researchers defined prose literacy as the skills needed to search and use information from continuous texts. Examples of continuous texts are news stories, brochures, and editorials. Document literacy was defined as the skills needed to search and use information from texts such as food labels, job applications, payroll forms, maps, etc. Quantitative literacy consisted of the skills necessary to perform computations such as figuring a tip or balancing a checkbook. For the purpose of this book, primarily only the results regarding prose and document literacy will be presented in this chapter.

Four literacy levels were reported:
1. Below Basic – illiterate, very simple literacy skills;
2. Basic – able to perform "everyday" activities;
3. Intermediate – able to perform somewhat challenging activities;
4. Proficient – able to perform complex literacy activities.

Scores ranged from 0 to 500.

The data were analyzed for literacy differences using many different characteristics, not just race and ethnicity. I present just a few of the results here and refer you to the actual report for a more complete analysis.

There was a significant difference in the percentage of White inmates who were Proficient in all three literacy areas as contrasted with the White household adults. Seven percent of the prison population scored Proficient in prose literacy, whereas 17% of household adults scored at the Proficient level. Although only 3% of White prison inmates were Proficient in document literacy, 15 % of White household adults were Proficient.

Nine percent and 6% of the White inmate population scored Below Basic for prose and document literacy, respectively, whereas 7% and 8% of household adults scored Below Basic in prose and document literacy, respectively. White inmates also had significantly lower average scores in all three assessed literacy areas than White household adults. The White inmates, however, had significantly higher average scores in the three areas than African American and Latino inmates.

In contrast, African American inmates had a higher average score (252) in prose literacy than African American household adults (243). There was no significant difference in the other two forms of literacy between inmates and household adults. One percent of the inmate population scored Proficient in prose whereas 2% of household adults were Proficient. For document literacy, 1% of the inmate population scored at the Proficient level, whereas 2% of household adults were Proficient. Fifteen percent and 19% of African American inmates scored Below Basic in prose and document literacy, respectively. Among household adults, 24% scored Below Basic for both prose and document literacy. Forty-nine percent of African American inmates and 47% of household adults scored Below Basic in quantitative literacy. Obviously, White inmates demonstrated higher scores in the three areas of literacy than African American household adults.

What do these differences mean? Without (or perhaps even with) further investigation, I can only speculate. On June 30, 2007, 46.4 % of the 208,300 women in local jails and state and federal prisons were White, 32.5 % African

American, and 15.4 % Latina. On the same date, of the approximately 2.1 million men in local jails and state and federal prisons, 35.4% were African American, 32.9% were White males, and 17.9% were Latino. This means that on this date, the American prison population comprised the following incarceration rates by race and gender: 4.6% of all African American men and .35% of all African American women; 1.7% of all Latino men and .15% of all Latina women; and .77% of all White men and .095% of all White women (Sabol & Couture, 2008). Perhaps if the literacy scores of African Americans in the general population equaled that of Whites in the general population, the African American incarceration rates might also be lower.

I am certainly not saying that literacy is the only factor to be considered. According to Human Rights Watch, an organization focused on protecting citizenry rights throughout the world, "African Americans are arrested, prosecuted, and imprisoned for drug offenses at far higher rates than whites. This racial disparity bears little relationship to racial differences in drug offending" (Human Rights Watch, 2003). There may also be factors related to mandatory sentencing, family composition (e.g., whether the family is headed by two parents), religious beliefs, racism in the judicial system (SPLC seeks justice, 2007), prosecutorial misconduct (Gaines, 2007), and a host of other factors at work that help to create and maintain this disparity.

Although this book does not focus on individuals with disabilities, it should be noted that 17% of the prison population had learning disabilities. In contrast, 6% of the household population had a learning disability (Greenberg, Dunleavy, & Kutner, 2007).

Literacy levels may also affect the inmates upon their return to society. The National Institute of Justice listed low literacy as one reason why former inmates are unemployed one year after release from prison (A Second Chance, 2004). Consequently, advocates promote literacy programs for inmates (Vacca, 2004).

There is also concern for the children of inmates. A library in Oregon collaborated with the sheriff's department to develop a parent education class for inmates regarding literacy development (Arnold & Colburn, 2006). Course instructors suggested books they could read to their children, and the inmates read the books. One inmate reported that he read his first entire book during the course.

Literacy may be a factor in decreasing our crime rate and subsequently our prison population. If reading can play a role in preventing a young person from committing a crime, we can ill afford to ignore it.

Chapter 6

Profiles of African American Examinees
Who Excelled Above the Mean

In this chapter, I profile 4 African American students, who scored above the mean on standardized tests. These students were Suzette, Chad, LaKeisha, and William. I focus specifically on their reading experiences prior to age 18. Data were collected from questionnaires, and additional questions (regarding family socioeconomic status, number of children in the family, preparatory courses taken, and information about high school) were asked through e-mail. William's mother completed his questionnaire, and William responded directly to follow-up questions via e-mail. Suzette is an elementary school student. Her mother completed her questionnaire and responded to additional questions via e-mail. Due to the passage of time, 2 of the 4 (Chad and LaKeisha) had difficulty specifying the quantities of books read or the exact amount of time spent reading. For this reason, I found their answers to question #8 to be more insightful.

Pseudonyms are used instead of real names. The questionnaire appears in Appendix A.

Suzette

Suzette's Iowa Test of Basic Skills Scores (third grade), September 2007			
	Percentile	Stanine	Grade Equivalent
Vocabulary	84	7	4.4
Reading Comprehension	91	8	5.4
Reading Total	89	8	4.8
Language Total	98	9	6.0
The Language total comprised spelling, capitalization, punctuation, usage, and expression.			
Math Total	83	7	4.0
The Math total comprised concepts and estimation, problem solving and data interpretation, and math computation.			
Core Total	95	8	4.8
The Core total represents the scores for Reading, Language, and Mathematics.			
Social Studies	83	7	4.4
Science	89	8	5.1
Sources of Information	87	7	4.6
The Sources of Information total reflects questions about maps, diagrams, and reference materials.			
Composite Score	93	8	4.7
The composite score comprised the scores for Reading, Language, Mathematics, Social Studies, and Science.			

Profiles of African American Examinees Who Excelled Above the Mean

The Iowa Test of Basic Skills is a norm-referenced test, i.e., individual student scores are compared to the norm group. The test developers administer the test to a sample of students who represent the examinees for whom the test was designed (McLoughlin & Lewis, 2008). This sample is the norm group.

A percentile score of 93 means that Suzette scored the same as or better than 93 percent of the children in the norm group for the test. Stanines (standard nines) range from one to nine. Stanines of one to three are below average. A stanine score of four is low average; a five is average; and a six is high average. Stanines of seven to nine represent above average scores (Pearson Educational Measurement, n.d.).

I encourage parents to rely on percentiles and stanines as opposed to grade equivalents for several reasons, which I will not explain in this book. Parents should keep in mind that just because a student receives a certain grade equivalent that is higher than the child's actual grade, it does not mean that the child should do the course work of that higher grade equivalent. Therefore, if your child is in the fourth grade and receives a grade equivalent score equal to the sixth grade in math, it does not mean that your child is ready for sixth grade math.

Suzette received these scores when she was eight years old and just beginning the third grade. Suzette lives with her mother and grandmother in an apartment.

Her mother, Sharon, was a student in two of my graduate-level courses. A teacher in the public school system, she is working on her master's degree. Sometimes Sharon would bring Suzette to class with her. While Sharon was doing class work, Suzette would read Harry Potter books. I suspected that Suzette's standardized test scores were above average just based on what I saw her reading in class. Without even knowing Suzette's scores, I decided to ask Sharon if I could profile her for this book. Once I received Suzette's scores on the Iowa Test of Basic Skills, my beliefs were confirmed.

I like to explain to my students the importance of reading, and I always give them a reading pledge to sign (see Appendix B). After I spoke about this issue in one class, Sharon raised her hand and indicated that she agreed with me. She stated that she once had a White roommate who had a baby. She noticed that every night, her roommate would read the book *Goodnight Moon* (Brown, 2005) to her baby. Sharon said she noticed that at some point, the baby seemed to try to read along with his mother. Sharon was impressed with what she saw and decided there and then that she would also read to her baby every night once she was born.

Sharon estimated that she read to her daughter approximately six times per week, beginning when she was born. Sharon reported that the A-Beka curriculum was used to teach Suzette to read at age four. This curriculum places an emphasis on phonics. Sharon also taught her daughter phonetic principles at the same time.

Suzette reads for pleasure during the school year. Sharon and Suzette's teacher require that she reads for at least 45 minutes each day after school. Sharon estimated that Suzette watches one to two hours of television per night, but only after her 45 minute reading period has been completed. She also stated that sometimes Suzette reads for more than 45 minutes. There are three computers in the apartment and Suzette has access to all of them.

Suzette's bedtime is at 9 p.m. every night, and the actual time Suzette gets into the bed varies between 8:45 p.m. and 9:15 p.m. Sharon said that Suzette listens to the same music that she enjoys, which is mainly gospel, jazz, R&B, and neo-soul music. Suzette does not listen to rap music or watch rap videos at home, although she may sometimes hear a rap song on the radio while they are in the car.

Suzette's school has the Accelerated Reader program, and Suzette reads books through the program. At the end of third grade, Suzette had the third highest number of Accelerated Reader points for the entire third grade and the fifth highest number of points for the entire school. She was the only African American among the 10 students in the entire school with the highest number of Accelerated Reader points. Although she does not participate in library summer reading programs, Sharon estimates that Suzette reads 50 books per summer that are more than 100 pages in length.

The student body population at her public elementary school is 49% African American, 32% White, 7% Latino, 8% multiracial, and 4% Asian. Approximately 47% of the students are eligible for free or reduced lunch.

Suzette makes all A's in school. Sharon believes that Suzette's reading ability has helped her in all her classes. When she grows up, Suzette wants to pursue a career as a writer or an actor.

Chad

A Comparison of Chad's Verbal Score with Other GRE Examinees

Chad's GRE Verbal Score: 540 in 1997

White GRE Verbal Mean in 1996: 496 (Grandy, 1999)

GRE Verbal Mean for all Examinees in 1997: 472 (Digest of Education Statistics, n.d.)

African American GRE Verbal Mean in 1996: 389 (Grandy, 1999). Group mean scores for the various ethnic groups in 1997 could not be obtained. Increases or decreases in scores from one year to the next are usually not huge.

Chad's mother and grandmother reared him and a younger brother in a large western city. His mother was a postal worker, and his grandmother was a domestic house cleaner. Chad believes that the combined income of his mother and grandmother placed their family in the low to middle-income range.

Although Chad said he was not read to as a child, he stated that his grandmother was a storyteller and spent hours telling him about her life growing up in the South. She told him that she did not have electricity in her childhood home and that she read by the fireplace. Chad believes that the story of her reading by the fireplace inspired him to read.

He attended public schools from kindergarten through third grade and Catholic schools from fourth through twelfth grade. The student population in his all-male high school was predominantly African American and middle-income.

Chad described himself as an "avid" reader during elementary school. He often ordered books to read. His teacher distributed book order forms; he paid her and the books arrived about three weeks later.

Chad also wrote the following on his questionnaire:

> Reading for pleasure went completely out the window when puberty hit. Although reading for pleasure during adolescence stopped, I was fortunate to have a very good English lit teacher for two years during high school. He was a young White guy who had a reputation for being a hard teacher. His class was great. He exposed my classmates and me to the great African American writers, Toni Morrison, Ralph Ellison, Richard Wright, and Alice Walker. We also were exposed to other great books such as *The Catcher in the Rye*, *A Tale of Two Cities*, etc.

Profiles of African American Examinees Who Excelled Above the Mean

I credit my love of writing to him, but of course I credit my love for books to my grandmother. (Chad, personal communication, July 20, 2007)

He purchased one GRE preparation book. He thought it was helpful in explaining how to take the test.

Chad has one graduate degree and is currently pursuing a second graduate degree. Although he is a full-time student now, he previously was employed as a public school teacher. He passed all his teaching certification exams (standardized tests) the first time he took them.

LaKeisha

A Comparison of LaKeisha's SAT Verbal Score with College-Bound Seniors in 1997
LaKeisha's SAT Verbal Score: 650
White Mean Verbal Score: 526
Mean Verbal Score for All Groups: 505
African American Mean Verbal Score: 434 (Source, 1997 Background Information; www.collegeboard.com)

LaKeisha was born in a midwestern state. Her mother, who subsequently divorced LaKeisha's father, moved with LaKeisha and her younger brother to a southern state. LaKeisha's mother was a hair stylist, and LaKeisha described their socioeconomic status as low-income.

African Americans and Standardized Tests

LaKeisha always attended public schools. She graduated in 1997 from a high school that was 51% White, 39% African American, and 9% other (all percentages rounded off). Some 19% of the students were eligible for free or reduced lunch.

Although LaKeisha's mother read to her infrequently, perhaps once or twice a week, she still learned to read at an early age, read a lot independently, and read "innumerable" books prior to entering first grade. She stated that reading was her hobby and her passion and that her mother was also a "big reader."

During her elementary school years, she participated in summer reading programs sponsored by libraries or other organizations. She also continued to read for pleasure during her middle-school and high-school years.

LaKeisha did not purchase any study materials or take any courses in preparation for the SAT. She had only the regular materials sent out to all registrants.

LaKeisha wrote the following on her questionnaire:

> Reading was always held in high regards in my family. I grew up watching my mom read. I can recall going to book exchange events and stores where we bought and traded books as our form of weekend recreation. I have never had problems reading and I began reading for fun at a very early age.
>
> Along with the support at home, I attended schools that stressed the importance of reading. I was blessed to be in classes with teachers who made us functional library users. I cannot

94

pinpoint the precise reason for my love of reading. I can only express how much I have always enjoyed it.

I believe being introduced to various genres of reading played a key role in my verbal test scores. Reading advanced literature at an early age introduced me to a broad range of vocabulary which increased my verbal scores. Reading advanced-level mysteries enhanced my critical thinking abilities. (LaKeisha, personal communication, August 29, 2007)

LaKeisha has a master's degree and is currently working on an Ed.S. degree. She is employed as a public school teacher. She passed all her teaching certification exams the first time she took them. She was exempt from taking a basic skills exam required of all teachers because of her high school SAT score.

William

A Comparison of William's SAT Critical Reading Score with Other 2007 College-Bound Seniors
William's SAT Critical Reading Score: 780
White SAT Critical Reading Mean Score: 527
SAT Critical Reading Mean Score for All Examinees: 502
African American SAT Critical Reading Mean Score: 433
William's SAT History Subject Test Score: 800

African Americans and Standardized Tests

A Comparison of William's ACT Reading Score with Other 2007 College-Bound Seniors
William's ACT Reading Score: 32
White ACT Reading Mean Score: 22.5
ACT Reading Mean Score for All Examinees: 21.5
African American ACT Reading Mean: 17.1

Although William, an only child, was born in a northern city, he was reared in the South. His mother, Connie, and his father divorced when William was a toddler. He had almost no contact with his father and did not see him again until he was 14. Connie stated that from age 14 to 18, William saw his father six times for no more than a few hours each time. William once laughed and told his mother, "I don't know that man." William's father also did not pay child support. Connie has several graduate degrees and his father did not finish college. Connie's yearly income is about $50,000, although it was in the $40,000 range for most of the years prior to William reaching 18 years of age.

Connie's motto is, "The family that reads together, achieves together." Therefore, she began to read to William when he was a few days old. She or other family members read to him at least one story each day. Connie purchased books for him via a children's book club. She also made regular biweekly trips to the library, checking out about 10 to 14 books at a time. At about two or three years of age, William began to participate in the summer reading programs sponsored by the local public library. Either he read for himself or family members read to him more than 2,000 books by the time he started first grade.

When William was 5 years old, his mother paid for him to take computer science lessons. When he was 6 years old, his grandparents bought him a computer. The computer was in his mother's bedroom until he was about a sophomore in high school when it was moved to his bedroom.

In the first grade, he participated in the Accelerated Reader program and had the second highest number of points in his school at the end of the year, having read more than 200 non-chapter books. At the beginning of fifth grade, he asked his mother for a Nintendo or a Play Station. She told him if he read 200 books of at least 100 pages during the academic year, she would buy him the game of his choice. He read the books and she bought the game.

William routinely read over 100 books a year (usually more than 200 pages in length) until about the eighth grade. (His mother kept a record of his reading until the eighth grade.) During his freshman and sophomore years, he read on average about two books a week, each with at least 200 pages. During his junior and senior years, he read about one book a week. He read at least 1,000 books, each with at least 200 pages, by the time he finished high school. Connie said at one time he owned about 400 books, before she started giving them away to other parents.

Connie said an acquaintance of hers had a son who graduated from a parochial school. The entire school took the SAT each year beginning in the seventh grade. Connie decided that William should take the test in seventh grade as well.

The first time he took the SAT in the seventh grade, William scored 600 on the Critical Reading section. As a result of his score, he was able to attend special summer programs at a highly selective university. He took the SAT again in the ninth, eleventh, and twelfth grades. William took the ACT for the first time in the tenth grade and again in the eleventh and twelfth grades. Connie purchased several SAT and ACT preparation books during his junior year. He also took a short (a few half-days) ACT course the summer between his junior and senior years that cost less than $100. When asked whether the course help him, he responded, "Not much" (William, personal communication, September 25, 2007.)

During middle school and high school, William participated in extracurricular activities. He participated in sports in middle school and was on two athletic teams during high school.

Connie said she never restricted his television watching and could not give an estimation of how much time he watched per day. She said she was not really concerned with that, as long as she knew he was reading. Although she had established bedtimes, she said William often ran behind schedule. William listened to all types of music, including rap. He did not, however, listen to a lot of "gangsta" rap. William reported via e-mail that he probably watched rap videos almost every day until about his sophomore year of high school.

Some 47% of the students at William's public high school were eligible for free or reduced-price lunch. His 2007 graduating class was approximately 50% African American, 42% White, and 8% Latino and other ethnic groups. The SAT Critical Reading mean score of his 2007 high-school class was 451. The ACT Reading mean score was 17. A public foundation in his state ranked William's high school as being in the bottom fourth of all the schools in the state in academic achievement.

William is currently in college. He receives a substantial need-based scholarship.

Discussion

These four profiled individuals share certain similarities in their backgrounds. For example, family members influenced them to read for pleasure. Each of them came from a middle-class family or attended a middle-class school. All four of them, to varying degrees, read more than what was required of them for school.

Another commonality is the fact that they were reared by single mothers, with three of the mothers receiving some type of assistance from a parent or parents. This fact is significant to me because I once taught at a predominantly White university where a White female student believed that only two-parent families were "good families" and firmly expressed this opinion in class. When another White female student tried to tell her that although a single-parent household may not be the ideal, it could still be a good family, the first White female completely rejected this idea. I suggested that as teachers, instead of counting the adults in the household, they should examine the family dynamics and look at what is happening in the family. I suggested that having a two-parent family where one family member is abusing alcohol or a spouse might be a worse situation for a child than a single-parent family. She seemed to reject this notion as well. I wondered how she would treat a poor African American student from a single-parent household.

Some of the students that I taught at that particular university seemed to think that they could use the family as an excuse not to do their jobs as teachers. If the family wasn't "good" or intact, or if there were other problems, well, what could teachers do? For the sake of Suzette, Chad, LaKeisha, William, and many other diligent African American students like them, this attitude troubles me. How would they have been treated by teachers who were biased against families headed by single females?

Chad and LaKeisha noted the impact that teachers had on their literacy skills. Whether students come from families that are single parent or intact, low-income or middle-class, teachers can still provide a positive influence on their reading habits. If you are a teacher with a strong bias against single-parent, low-income, and/or culturally and linguistically diverse families, I humbly implore you to leave the teaching profession immediately or seek employment where you will only teach children from intact, middle-class families of your preferred ethnic group. You know who you are.

Chapter 7

Using Common Sense

College professors and research scientists should skip this chapter. It was not written for you. No insult is intended, but you want research to support every statement. Although I believe I have already presented enough research to support this chapter, inasmuch as "common sense" is the operative phrase, it is probably best if you just skip the chapter.

I'm sure you have heard the expression "Practice makes perfect." Constantly doing a certain activity, such as playing the piano or playing basketball, will improve your skills. Now think about taking standardized tests. Written standardized tests do not require that you sing, dance, play the piano, or shoot basketballs. You read. It should come as no surprise that people who "practice" reading a lot (and comprehend what is read) score higher on tests that involve reading (Gambrell, 2007; Topping, Samuels, & Paul, 2007; National Endowment for the Arts, 2007) than people of equal intellect who read less.

For example, if you have two basketball players of equal ability and one practices a lot and the other doesn't, you would expect the one who practices more to perform better. Even professional basketball players are expected to practice. Why should reading be any different? Sometimes when I see young African American males playing basketball hour after hour, I find myself thinking, "I hope they spend half as much time reading."

Exercising is another good example. People who lift weights every day will probably have stronger muscles than people who do not. Tim Green, a former National Football League (NFL) player, now an attorney, television commentator, and author, encourages children to read. He says that reading is like "exercise for the mind" (Ryan, 2007, p. E2.).

Expensive preparation courses do not guarantee that students will score well on standardized tests. Preparation for taking standardized tests is a lifelong process that begins at birth, not at age 16. Perhaps an analogy for reading can be made using golf. The father of pro golfer, Eldrick "Tiger" Woods, did not give Tiger his first golfing lesson when he was 16. Tiger first imitated his father's golf swing when he was six months old. He was putting on national television with Bob Hope when he was two (About Tiger, n.d.). Now if you can afford to spend money on an expensive preparation course for your child, by all means do it, but don't view it as an adequate substitute for lifelong learning and reading.

I once had an African American student in graduate school who did not accept my assertion that a lack of reading depressed the scores of African Americans. She said, "It ["it" being the cause of lower scores] is something else." She could not tell me what "it" was. She said, "When I took the [college admission] tests, how was I supposed to know the meaning of words like 'incredulous'?" Incredulous is the exact word she used in her example. I did not ask her whether the word actually gave her difficulty or whether she was just using it as an example. I remember thinking, "Are you serious? You didn't know the meaning of incredulous?" I didn't have the heart to tell her that if she had read more, she probably would have come across the word and would have known its meaning when she took the test.

Once while at the library, I listened to a young White adolescent male as he talked to the librarian. A sophomore in high school, he said he was thinking about joining the Navy after graduation. I glanced at the ten or so books he was checking out, and they all seemed to be novels for pleasure reading, although they could have been for school assignments. I have no way of knowing for sure. I remember thinking that if he were to take the test for the Navy, he would probably score higher than other young men of equal intellect but who had read a great deal less. He made no mention of even considering going to college. He was with an older woman and a younger boy, about four years old. The four year old also had about ten books and appeared to struggle a little under the weight of them. I remember thinking, "This is how White people from a certain income status outscore African Americans from a higher socioeconomic class."

It's been said that "reading is the great equalizer." I cannot tell you who said it first, but I can explain what it means. Reading exposes you to places you never knew existed and ideas you never considered. Even though you may lack the resources of a middle or upper-income family, reading can help to level the playing field. A lack of reading can create a deficit in your knowledge-base and awareness of all that the world has to offer.

Let me give you an example of how reading can serve as an equalizer. Perhaps a child knows and uses the word "umbrella," but does not know or use the word "parasol." Moreover, the people in the child's immediate environment do not use "parasol." If the child doesn't know the meaning of "parasol" and takes a test where "parasol" is used, the child may get the answer to the question wrong. Now imagine another child in the same community who also only uses the word "umbrella," but who knows the meaning of the word "parasol" from reading various books. If the second child takes a test and the word "parasol" is used instead of "umbrella," that word substitution alone will not cause the child to get the answer wrong. Answering one question correctly may make the difference between receiving a passing score on a test necessary for some type of certification, job, or admission to a university program—and failing.

I can give you another example that actually occurred when I taught in the public schools of New York City. A speech therapist was talking to a student about needles from pine trees when it became apparent that the only needle the student knew about was the type used in a hypodermic syringe. Reading could have exposed the child to the existence of other types of needles.

Reading can help make the experiences of the economically disadvantaged closer to the experiences of the middle-class and beyond. William, who was profiled in the last chapter, is from a middle-income family, headed by a single mother who makes approximately $50,000. His SAT Critical Reading score of 780, however, was higher than the mean score of Asian American students from families making more than $100,000 a year (568) and their White counterparts (548). William's score was also higher than the mean score of Asian seniors (574) and White seniors (570) from families where the highest level of parental education was a graduate degree. William's mother believed that reading put her son on the level of a child who had attended exclusive private schools. For William, reading was the great equalizer.

Some of you may question my assertion that the lack of long-term reading affects the scores of African Americans on standardized tests. Well, let's say I am wrong. So what if I am? What harm can be done by reading to your children every day, beginning when they are infants? What harm can be done by requiring them to read 30 minutes a day for pleasure (reading what they want to read, with parental supervision) when they are older? Now, let's say that I am correct, and you do not read daily to your children beginning when they are infants and you do not encourage your children to read more than what is required for school. What harm can be done to your children then? If I am wrong, I am only suggesting that African American parents err on the side of caution.

Chapter 8

What Can We Do? It May Take a Village

You have probably heard of the African (Yoruba language) proverb that "It takes a village to raise [rear] a child." It very well may take a village to effectuate widespread change in the African American community regarding reading and consequently, academic achievement (Ferguson, 2005). In one research project, different community members were asked to promote reading (Edwards, 1992).

Based on a review of the literature regarding reading, I have compiled the following recommendations for the various people (parents, educators, etc.) who play a role in children's literacy development.

Recommendations for Parents

Begin reading to your baby on the day your child is born or as soon as you can afterwards (Hall, 2001). Please do not wait until the child is one year old. Try to read at least one short story each day of the week. If you have the time, try reading at least three different stories (non-chapter books) per day. If three stories are read each day, your child will have had more than 6,000 books read to him by the time he enters first grade. In addition to reading different books, it is also acceptable to read some of the same stories (especially your child's favorites) over and over again (Honig, 2004).

Read books with rhymes to your infant (Sullivan, 2005). Cardboard books are quite durable and can be used with infants. You can also purchase waterproof books which you can keep near the bathtub (Straub, 2006). Spiral bound books are not recommended for infants (Honig, 2004).

You should also speak directly to your child each day. Some researchers have suggested that infants and toddlers need to hear 30,000 words per day ("Young Children Thrive," 2008).

As the child gets older, ask open-ended questions (Association for Library Service to Children, 2003) about the stories you're reading, and make comments as you read them (Honig, 2004). For example, if there is a blue car in the book and your child has a cousin with a blue car, you can say, "Your cousin has a blue car" (Ard & Beverly, 2004; Hockenburger, Goldstein, & Haas, 1999).

Do not feel that you have to purchase these books. Go to the library on a regular basis and check out enough books to last for a week or two. The library can give you access to more books than you can buy (unless you are extremely wealthy). Please do not think that the books you have in your house are sufficient. They are only sufficient if you supplement them with books from the library. Senator Hillary Clinton stated in her autobiography that her mother took her to the library every week (Clinton, 2003). Evidently, Senator Clinton's mother did not believe she had enough books in her house, and neither should you.

If and when you purchase books for your infants and toddlers, I suggest you select interactive books (Honig, 2004). These books engage the child by causing him to perform some action. Examples of interactive books are those that have pop-up pages or that cause the child to move a lever on the page, which might reveal a hidden illustration.

What Can We Do? It May Take a Village

Make sure that your child participates in summer reading programs, which are sponsored by many local public libraries (Cech, 2007). These programs often give away prizes and even clothing to encourage participation. Check with your local library to see what programs are offered throughout the year, and try to involve your child in as many activities as possible.

During summer vacation, if your child is reading short, non-chapter story books, have him read at least three books a day. If your child is reading chapter books, have him read at least 50 books during summer vacation. Some school systems have year-round school, with several short breaks during the academic year. Therefore, if a child is reading chapter books, I suggest that approximately 100 books with at least 100 pages each be read in a year. This averages out to about 27 pages a day.

Another approach would be to have your child read 30 minutes a day, every day. This suggestion is based on Fischgrund's research (2004). He found that students in the control group who scored at least average on the SAT read for pleasure about four hours a week. Reading for 30 minutes a day equals 3.5 hours of reading per week. If your child wants to attend a highly selective university or become a doctor, he should read even more. Please do not think this is too much reading or that there's not enough time in the day. What is your child doing while sitting in a car, bus, subway train, or doctor's office? Instead of watching TV or playing a video game, your child could read a book.

At least occasionally, your elementary school age children should read aloud to you. Former presidential candidate John Edwards' 8-year-old son read aloud to his mother for an hour each day ("Report," 2008). Initially, you should monitor the number of errors young readers make. Experts suggest that by the end of first, second, and third grades, students should be able to read correctly 50, 90, and 110 words a minute, respectively (Chute, 2007).

If your child's school has Accelerated Reader, make sure he participates. Accelerated Reader (www.renlearn.com/ar/overview) is a reading practice software program used in thousands of schools. Students read books and take quizzes. The software program corrects the quizzes and gives the teacher and students feedback about the results. The Scholastic Company produces Reading Counts, which is a similar software program (teacher.scholastic.com/products/readingcounts/).

Jet magazine (Waldron, 2007) featured an article about a 7-year-old African American boy who read 330 books as a first grader. The child's teacher asked all of the students to read for at least 30 minutes after completing homework. The teacher noticed that the students' reading improved and then told them that the student who read the most books would receive a prize. The boy was the child of a single mother, and his father was deceased. I share this story so that African American parents will know what is possible.

If you have older children who have not developed a habit of reading, help them find books that interest them. Do not force them to read books they find boring (Ryan, 2007). You may have to require that they read less than 30 minutes per day, gradually building up to at least 30 minutes. Explain to them why you are instituting this requirement. Appendix C contains an annotated bibliography of books your children might find interesting.

What Can We Do? It May Take a Village

Recommendations for Educators

If your school has Accelerated Reader or a similar program, make sure each student in your class participates. According to the Web site about Accelerated Reader, it is supported by research and meets the requirements of No Child Left Behind (www.renlearn.com/ar/overview). Some researchers have stated that Accelerated Reader uses incentives or rewards (Melton, et al., 2004). The Web site for Accelerated Reader does not mention incentives or rewards as a component or requirement for the implementation of the program. School personnel, on their own initiative, may have started offering incentives to encourage student participation.

I do not advocate tying Accelerated Reader to grades, unless it is for extra credit or bonus points. Students should select books they want to read. In one study, high-school students complained that a portion of their English grade was based on their Accelerated Reader quizzes and that they were required to read books that did not interest them. Unfortunately, some of the students resorted to cheating on the Accelerated Reader tests. The researcher had not planned to ask the students about reading, but the students felt strongly about their problems with their Accelerated Reader experiences and wanted their viewpoints heard (Thompson, 2007).

Recognize that for some children, the only reading they may do is what you require of them. This is especially true if you are teaching in a low-income area. If students are reading short, non-chapter books, try to require that they read at least one book a day.

If you're teaching at the elementary level, try to have an extensive library within your own classroom. Ask friends, churches, and other organizations to donate books for use in your classroom. I've only toured one exclusive (i.e., expensive) private school in my life. I was surprised at the number of books in each lower-grade classroom. There were at least 300 books for pleasure reading in each classroom. The school library looked like the branch location of a well-funded public library.

In one school district, parents are encouraged to come to school prior to the Christmas holidays to read their favorite Christmas books to the students (Ivey, 2007). I realize that depending on the political environment of a particular community, reading certain Christmas books might pose problems for teachers. Therefore, I would modify this activity and suggest that parents be encouraged to come in and read teacher-selected books. Although you may think the parents in your school district may be unwilling to do so, you will never know until you ask them.

Some teachers are using interactive books that incorporate technology. One educator described the use of LeapFrog School House books. While reading the books, students touch the word with a stylus and the audio component of the book will say and define the word (Mollin, 2005).

If your older students are reading chapter books, try to get them to read a book a week. Obviously, the required number of books per week depends on the length of the book. Have students read at least 25–30 pages a day or for 30 minutes a day. Fischgrund (2004) found that the students in the control group on average read 4 hours per week in connection with school assignments.

Consider using sustained silent reading (SSR) if your school will allow it. There is some controversy regarding SSR. The National Reading Panel reviewed the available research and concluded that there was not enough research to prove that independent, silent reading improved reading fluency or other reading skills (National Reading Panel, 2000). They emphasized that it does not mean that the practice is not beneficial, just that it cannot be proven from the available research. They said SSR should not be used as the sole reading instructional strategy. (I would never recommend that SSR be used as the only reading instructional strategy, nor have I ever met a teacher who used it as the sole strategy.) Consequently, because of the findings of the National Reading Panel, some school officials may discourage SSR.

Others disagree with the conclusions of the Panel. Krashen (2006, 2007) argued that there was a tremendous amount of research to support SSR. Although newer SSR models incorporate discussion as a component, he still felt that the older model of SSR was beneficial.

Bylut Ermitage and Van Slurp (2007) interviewed 25 third-grade students to determine their opinions regarding SSR. The students were asked, "What is happening for you during SSR?" Thirty-two percent answered, "Just reading." Follow-up questioning clarified "just reading." Students meant that they had no further academic demands placed on them, such as writing a report. Twenty-four percent said they were learning. Sixteen percent said they were having fun. Twelve percent said they appreciated the silence, and 28% said they made decisions about what to read, where to sit, etc. The researchers recommended that teachers allocate time for discussion of what was read.

In order to minimize resistance to reading, especially among students who have not read a lot at home, tell students why you are requiring them to read. This may not work with every student, but you may be able to help some of them understand its importance.

You must be very careful how you talk to students. When talking to younger children you can say, "Oh, I'm so proud of you. You're such smart little girls and boys. Let me tell you how you can score even higher on all the tests you must take. You have to read a lot, but we're going to make it fun." You will have to use your professional judgment as to how you make reading fun.

Making reading fun relates to the issue of motivation. Edmunds and Bauswerman (2006) studied reading motivation in fourth-grade students. These students attended a school where 74% of students received free or reduced lunch. Children were asked about their motivation to read. Based on their answers, the researchers identified several categories of motivation. Students said they were motivated by family members (mostly the mother), teachers, and the children themselves. One factor that influenced children to read narrative texts was personal interest. A factor that motivated children to read expository texts was the belief that they would gain knowledge.

If you have older students you can say,

"For those of you going to college, your scores on standardized tests can help determine what school you attend. Doing as much reading as possible will help you when you take these tests. People who read more do better on tests. For those of you who plan to attend technical school, the reading you do now will help you comprehend the written materials you will encounter in school. If you plan to go into the military after high school, you will probably have to take some type of written test. Your score on the test could help decide your occupation in the military and affect your enlistment bonus. So, it's important that you do well. For those of you who plan to play in the National Basketball Association (NBA), you can no longer go directly from high school to a professional team. You will need a certain score on the SAT or ACT in order to play your freshman year and therefore be able to show your skills to pro team recruiters. You should also have a Plan B, just in case you don't make it to the NBA. Being a good reader can enable you to finish college and pursue another career. If you plan to enter the entertainment business, being able to read well may lessen the chances of someone taking advantage of you. For that matter, you and students across the country have to take a standardized test in order to receive your high-school diploma. (Make this statement if it is true for the students in your state.) Reading can help all of you achieve your goals."

These statements have to be made over and over again.

In addition, some students may not even attempt to perform well on standardized tests, believing the tests to be insignificant and "a waste of time" (Thompson, 2007, p. 72). The above statements explain to students why standardized tests are important and how the tests can affect their lives.

Your interpersonal relationships with students may also affect their performance on standardized tests. One educator related the story of how one little African American boy refused to take a standardized test. When the principal, an African American male, attempted to coax the child into taking the test, the child responded, "I ain't giving that white woman one more reason to say I'm dumb" (Thompson, 2007, p. 182, 281). The White woman was his teacher. As an educator, try to be aware of the impact you can have on a student.

Explain to parents, adapting the above scripts, why it is so important that they encourage reading above and beyond what is required for school. Specify how many books you expect their children to read over the summer. Emphasize how important it is for them to read during the summer. Give the parents pledges to sign, in which they agree to read to their children each night or make sure that their children engage in pleasure reading each night for at least 30 minutes.

As a teacher, try to understand that no matter how low the socioeconomic status of the student population, there are always some students who are striving to excel academically. At one high school in Florida, 7 students joined together to develop their own SAT preparation course (Freedman, 2008). Half of the students at this high school qualified for free or reduced lunches. The students met 3 times a week for 90-minute sessions after school. These students would be receptive to increasing their reading volume (amount of reading) if they thought it would benefit them on their college admission tests.

Do not allow yourself to believe that you are powerless to effectuate change or motivate students to read (Anderson, Wilson, & Fielding, 1986; Edmunds and Bauswerman 2006). You may not be able to save every child, but you can possibly save one.

Recommendations for School Systems

Make sure your teachers understand the importance of encouraging students to read and how a lack of reading can detrimentally affect standardized test scores. Consider making Accelerated Reader, Reading Counts, or another reading practice software part of your curriculum.

Devise system-wide programs to encourage reading. At Parent Teacher Association meetings, always have presentations or discussions about the importance of reading. Tell parents that it is extremely important to read to their children, and give them the suggestions for parents from this book or a set of guidelines generated by professionals in the school system. Give them a specific suggested number of books for their children to read in the summer, or specify the amount of time to be spent on pleasure reading throughout the academic year and summer.

Tell parents that a lack of reading can detrimentally affect standardized test scores, and tell them about the implications of standardized tests for college admissions, jobs, playing sports at the college level, and the military.

It may even be necessary to devise training programs to develop parental book reading skills (Edwards, 1992; North & Allen 2005). One such program lasted for several months and consisted of coaching, peer modeling, and parent-child interactions (Edwards, 1992). During the parent-child interactions, the mothers read to the children while the instructor provided guidance and support.

One school has implemented monthly "Muffins with Moms" and "Donuts with Dads" sessions (Nelson, 2007). During these sessions, mothers, fathers, or their surrogates (such as an aunt or uncle) come to the school to read with their children prior to the start of the school day. The purpose is to give working parents, who may not have time to spend with their children at home, a designated time for reading. The sessions encourage parental involvement and demonstrate

115

to the children the importance of reading. The principal also stated that the sessions increased the children's self-esteem.

The Loudon County School System in Virginia uses the Steps to Literacy program to teach phonetics, vocabulary, word recognition, reading comprehension, fluency, spelling, and writing (Chandler, 2007). School system officials claim that the program has boosted the percentage of students in the district who meet designated goals in the state literacy test. The program is used in classrooms that reflect diversity in socioeconomic status, ethnicity, language, and academic ability. I suggest that other school district officials contact the Loudon County School System to obtain their research results regarding the program. School system personnel should consider adopting the program if the data indicate that it is more beneficial than the literacy-development curriculum they are currently using.

Some students in Kentucky are using a Web-based program that promotes literacy. School personnel say that the program, Achieve 3000, has helped their students to improve their reading comprehension skills (Parrino, 2008). They also contend that student behavior has improved. Again, if your program is not working, use a proven program that will.

School districts should consider starting a boys and/or girls club for students who are struggling academically. Schools in the Boston Public School System selected 10 males from each participating school to join a "10 Boys Club." The students received tutoring, had special lunches, and participated in activities with their principals. The purpose of the club was to foster academic achievement through peer, school, and parental support. In one year, at least half of the students advanced one level in the English or math Massachusetts Comprehensive Assessment System tests

(Tracy, 2007). I recommend that any such club put an emphasis on increasing the amount of students' pleasure reading.

School districts must determine how computers can be harnessed to improve literacy and enhance academic achievement. Some educators have predicted that by 2019, half of the courses for high school students will be delivered online (Christensen, Johnson, & Horn, 2008, as cited in Trotter, 2008).

South Carolina already appears to be headed in this direction. Three full-time, online or cyber schools were scheduled to be opened by fall 2008. Two of the schools will educate students from kindergarten through the 12th grade and a third will be for high school students. As of 2008, 18 states operated full-time cyber schools, and 38 states offered some online classes (Adcox, 2008). These virtual schools may have implications not only for improving literacy but for decreasing disciplinary problems and improving the recruitment and retention of teachers.

Recommendations for African American Greek Sororities and Fraternities

1. Make sure that every teacher you know has a well-stocked classroom library, preferably containing at least 300 books at the K–5 level. Offer to donate books to classrooms as part of a service project.
2. Try to think of service activities where you can incorporate a reading focus.
3. Make sure the children in your immediate family are doing enough pleasure reading.
4. Provide free tutoring in reading (or any other subject).

African Americans and Standardized Tests

Recommendations for Churches

Churches have an important role to play, especially if they are located in areas where the residents do not have ready access to libraries. Although some urban communities and rural areas may not have libraries that citizens can reach if they lack adequate transportation, churches in those communities may be more accessible. Some ministers have preached about the importance of reading and the role parents play in the development of literacy (Edwards, 1992).

1. Sponsor activities with a reading focus throughout the year.
2. Encourage students in the church to read during the summer. It is important to specify the number of books to be read, or specify the amount of time (30 minutes) to read each day.
3. Establish tutoring/mentoring programs. The programs should focus on increasing the mentees' pleasure reading.
4. Maintain a church library of books for children. Encourage parents to come in and read to their children before or after church activities. It is quite understandable that churches would not want to have some books in their libraries. Establish a library committee to review books before inclusion in the library.

Recommendations for Rappers/ Hip-Hop Artists, Athletes, and Other Entertainers

Entertainers and athletes have the power to reach people that may not read or hear about this book. You would not be alone in your outreach attempts. Deejay Ra, the owner of a Canadian entertainment company, has started a Hip-Hop

Literacy Campaign (Hip Hop Press, 2007). Different celebrities have taped public service announcements, encouraging children to read.

Celebrities have also volunteered in other literacy campaigns. American hip-hop artists/rappers LL Cool J, Wyclef Jean, and Lil Mama participated in the Jumpstart Read for the Record event to raise money for early childhood education programs. The artists read to children as part of the event (It's Hip to Read, 2007).

As I stated earlier in the book, BET aired a provocative animated video titled, "Read a Book" (Armah, 2007). It contained very crude language and I believe, based on news reports, that at least some African Americans did not view it as satire and focused instead on the vulgarity ("Read a Book Music Creators," 2007). I wish the rappers would band together to produce another rap song encouraging reading, without the profanity. Here are my other suggestions:

1. At your concerts, talk about the power of reading. Tell parents that if they want their children to do well in school, they must start reading to them at birth. Tell them to read a story a day.

2. For those of you who have foundations, give away free storybooks at your foundation sponsored activities.

3. When you visit schools, talk about the importance of reading. Offer the top five readers or more importantly, the five most-improved readers in a grade, the opportunity to have lunch with you.

4. Visit maternity wards of urban hospitals and give away free books. Encourage mothers to read to their children each night. If you cannot visit, collaborate with a hospital and donate books to mothers in your name or in the name of your foundation (North & Allen, 2005).

African Americans and Standardized Tests

Recommendations for Concerned Citizens

1. Visit inner city elementary classrooms to determine the amount of books in the classrooms. Offer to lead a book drive to bring more books into the classroom, or simply donate books.
2. Donate an old computer to an organization, such as Computer for Communities, that will give it to a low-income family.
3. Volunteer your time, donate books and/or money to literacy programs.
4. Inform friends and relatives about the importance of reading and its relationship to standardized test performance.

Recommendations for College Professors of Education

Preservice teachers should familiarize themselves with the research regarding reading, reading achievement, and standardized tests. They should have strategies for increasing the amount of K–12 student reading time. They should develop strategies for informing parents about the importance of reading, the minimum amount of daily pleasure reading children should do, and how reading can help children become productive citizens.

Explicitly discuss the theme of this book with your students. Make sure they understand the historical context in which the lack of widespread, long-term reading beginning during infancy occurred. Due to racial sensitivities, I recommend that non-African American professors emphasize that they are merely sharing the contents of a book that was written by an African American professor.

I teach graduate students in education at a historically Black university. I require that my students sign a pledge regarding reading. My latest version of the pledge is in Appendix B.

Chapter 9

Community Projects and Resources that Promote Reading

The following list of projects, programs, and resources promote literacy or academic achievement. Some parents may wish to use these resources. Others may wish to volunteer, donate money, or even develop their own literacy project.

Academic Talent Searches

If your child already scores exceptionally well on standardized tests, you may want to have him/her participate in an academic-talent program. The four universities that conduct major talent searches are Duke, Northwestern, Johns Hopkins, and the University of Denver. These institutions conduct talent searches for different grades, and you should check their Web sites to find out which university has the right talent search for your child's grade level.

The universities have divided the country into regions, and which talent search your child would participate in would depend on where you live. Check the Web sites to find out which university administers the talent search for your region. For example, as of 2008, students who live in California are in the region of Johns Hopkins University. Once a child has been identified, however, he/she may be able to participate in a program located in another region.

These institutions offer distance learning courses, independent study courses, travel abroad programs, and special summer programs. Duke University provides a directory of other universities that offer special programs for academically gifted children and youth.

www.du.edu/city
www.tip.duke.edu
www.cty.jhu.edu
www.ctd.northwestern.edu

AdLit.org

This project offers resources for parents and educators to enhance the literacy skills of children, grades 4–12. The Web site provides teaching strategies, research reports, tips for parents, and activities for children.

www.AdLit.org

American Library Association (ALA)

The Association for Library Service to Children (ALSC) is a division of the ALA and comprises librarians, literature experts, and educators. The online portal of this division features Web sites for children, booklists, resources for parents, and other helpful information.

www.ala.org

America's Literacy Directory

The directory provides a database of literacy programs, services, and activities located in the nation and U.S. territories. Some programs rely on volunteers, and most accept donations (often tax deductible).

www.literacydirectory.org

Community Projects and Resources That Promote Reading

Andre Agassi College Preparatory Academy

The retired professional tennis player, Andre Agassi, established this charter school in 2001 in Las Vegas, Nevada. It is located in a low-income area, and most of the students are African American. According to the Web site, the school features smaller classes and an extended school day. The parents pledge to read with their children for at least 20 minutes each night.

www.agassiprep.org

Book It! Program

The mission of this read-aloud program is to encourage reading. It provides free materials to teachers, suggestions for parents, and donates books to schools. The program starts on October 1 and ends on March 31 of each academic year. The program is supported by Pizza Hut, and if students meet the monthly reading goals established by their teachers, they can receive free pizzas. The program encourages students to read at least 20 minutes a day.

www.bookitprogram.com

Carver Academy

David Robinson, a former professional basketball player, and his wife founded this school named for the African American scientist, George Washington Carver. It is located in San Antonio, Texas. Generous scholarships are offered. The curriculum includes Accelerated Reader.

www.thecarveracademy.com

African Americans and Standardized Tests

Computers for Communities

Jacob Komar was 9 years old when he started this organization. Computers are refurbished and then given to children whose families cannot afford them. The main office is in Burlington, Connecticut. If someone needs a computer, he/she should contact the main office and an attempt will be made to put that person in contact with a local organization.

You can assist this organization by donating your time, skills, computers, or money. Donations are tax deductible. You can also start a local Computers for Communities organization with help from the main office.

> Computers for Communities
> P.O. Box 1203
> Burlington, CT 06013
> Phone: 860/656-7913
> computers4communities.org
> For computer donations: info@computers4 communities. org

Dolly Parton's Imagination Library

Dolly Parton established this organization in 1996 to promote reading among preschool children in her home county in Tennessee. The Library sends books to the children, and the program ends for them when they reach five years of age. Other communities now collaborate with the Dollywood Foundation to deliver books to preschool children in their communities.

www.dollysimaginationlibrary.com

Community Projects and Resources That Promote Reading

First Book

First Book has distributed more than 50 million books to literacy programs that serve low-income children. First Book joined with the U.S. Department of Education to create the Book Donation Campaign, which has several reading projects. First Book accepts donations and states on its Web site that every $2.50 donation purchases one book.
www.bookfirst.org

Harlem Children's Zone Inc. (HCZ Inc.)

The goal of this organization is to improve the lives of children through multifaceted programs. It serves approximately 10,000 at-risk children and their families in New York City. One project of HCZ Inc. is SMART (Shaping Minds Around Reading and Technology). SMART was developed to improve the reading skills of children through computer-based literacy programs. HCZ Inc. also lends books to children through its library program.
http://www.hcz.org

Kanye West Foundation

Rapper/hip-hop artist Kanye West established this organization to reduce the dropout rate in schools. One aim of the organization is to increase literacy. Loop Dreams, a rap-writing and music production program, is an initiative of the Foundation. West's mother, Dr. Donda West, a former college professor of English, served as Chair of the Board of Directors until her death in 2007 (Christian, 2007). The

Foundation is headquartered in Los Angeles and accepts tax-deductible contributions.

www.kanyewestfoundation.org

KIPP Schools

The Knowledge is Power Program (KIPP) comprises some 57 schools located throughout the country. Forty-eight of the schools serve students in the fifth through the eighth grades. Most are charter schools. Students are in school from 7:30 a.m. to 5:00 p.m. Monday through Friday and four hours on Saturdays. They also attend summer school for three to four weeks. The schools are tuition free, and students are accepted on a first-come basis. Ninety percent of the students are African American or Latino, and 80% are eligible for free or reduced lunch. Some of the students' standardized test results are posted on the Web site. Parents pledge to read with their children every night. Interested parties can donate money and/or time to KIPP schools.

www.kipp.org

The Ludacris Foundation

The Ludacris Foundation, founded by rapper/hip-hop artist Ludacris, focuses on the arts, health, education, individuals with disabilities, and provides assistance to families and grants to nonprofit organizations. It has supported the National Basketball Association's Read to Achieve Program in Atlanta. The foundation accepts tax-deductible donations.

www.theludacrisfoundation.org

Community Projects and Resources That Promote Reading

National Basketball Association Read to Achieve Program

This program promotes literacy and encourages parents to read to their children. Professional basketball players read to students in schools and at other events.
www.nba.com

National Education Association (NEA)

The NEA is a professional organization of educators. The NEA's Web site lists several books that teachers, celebrities, and children have recommended. The Web site also lists books by topic. For example, a state list features books that are relevant to each of the 50 states and Washington, DC. Read Across America, a project of the NEA, encourages reading among children. Read Across America partners with other organizations and projects that work to enhance the literacy skills of children and youth.
www.nea.org

One Laptop Per Child (OLPC)

OLPC's mission is to provide inexpensive laptop computers to children in underdeveloped countries. Sometimes OLPC has a special promotion in which a buyer can purchase two computers, one of which can be given to a child in another country. I suggest that you give the second computer to a needy child in this country or to an organization that will donate the computer to a needy child.
http://laptop.org

African Americans and Standardized Tests

Opportunity NYC

New York City has a program in which families receive financial incentives for completing certain tasks in education, health, and employment. It is based on the "conditional cash transfer model" that has been used in other countries. Conditional transfer programs provide monetary awards to individuals who behave in certain required ways (Janvry & Sadoulet, 2004). The program is administered only in certain communities, and families must have at least one child in the fourth, seventh, or ninth grade.

Several incentives are available. For example, a family can receive $50 for obtaining a library card. An increase in standardized test scores can result in an incentive payment of at least $300.

Although the program gives an incentive for obtaining a library card, obtaining a card does not guarantee that books are being read. Therefore, I suggest that the incentive be tied to actually reading books, if they are not already doing so now. Accelerated Reader or some other type of software program could be used to verify that the student has read a certain number of books.

Page Ahead

This Seattle-based organization provides free books and sponsors literacy activities for children from low-income families. Volunteers sponsor book drives or donate funds for the purchase of books.

http://pageahead.org

Community Projects and Resources
That Promote Reading

Reach Out and Read (ROR)

The mission of this organization is to promote literacy. ROR gives books to pediatricians who then give the books to their patients. The Web site states that research on the ROR model found that children who participated in ROR showed improvement in their language.

www.reachoutandread.org

Read to Me

This program encourages mothers, especially teen mothers, to read to their infants. The Web site provides tips, has a Frequently Asked Questions section, and suggests activities that mothers can do with their children.

www.readtomeprogram.org

Reading Education Assistance Dogs

In this program, children with reading difficulties practice reading aloud in a non-threatening environment where they will not fear the ridicule of their classmates. The children read to specially trained therapy dogs. Several organizations sponsor these programs, and you can find them by doing a Google search for "Reading Education Assistance Dogs."

www.therapyanimals.org/read/about.html

Reading Is Fundamental, Inc. (RIF)

A former teacher founded this organization in 1966 when she realized that some young children did not own books. RIF's mission is to promote literacy especially among children from birth through eight years old. RIF provides free books, sponsors online literacy contests, and other activities. It also operates the federally and privately funded Inexpensive Book Distribution Program for the U.S. Department of Education. The organization relies on more than 450,000 volunteers to perform various activities such as ordering books, reading to children, and organizing events. RIF accepts tax deductible donations.

www.rif.org

Ron Clark Academy

Ron Clark, a former winner of the Disney American Teacher Award, established a school for fifth through eighth grade students in Atlanta, Georgia. A goal of the school is for each student to receive an extensive four-year program. According to the Web site, the library is "breathtaking."

www.ronclarkacademy.com

School Evaluation/Ranking Web sites

Several Web sites provide information about schools and school districts and might include standardized test score results, school demographics, community demographics, parent ratings, and articles and information about parenting issues. The Web sites vary in the types of information given, so parents should do a thorough search. For example, one Web site may have no parent ratings for a particular school, whereas another will have parent ratings and comments.

www.education.com

www.greatschools.net

www.schoolmatters.com.

Tim Green's Reading Project for Kids

Tim Green is a former NFL player turned attorney, television celebrity, and author. He believes that children should read books that are fun and should not be forced to read books they find boring (Ryan, 2007). He speaks at schools to encourage reading and often waives his appearance fee, asking that the schools buy books with the money. Green wrote a book titled *Football Genius* aimed at 10 to 14 year olds. He has given away many copies of his book to children who cannot afford to purchase it.

www.timgreenbooks.com

Chapter 10

Final Thoughts

I understand that not every parent is trying to rear a child who will make a perfect SAT or ACT score. Many parents may simply wish to rear a happy, well-adjusted, well-rounded child who becomes a productive citizen of society. This indeed should probably be the ultimate goal of every parent.

When you consider, however, that some high schools are nicknamed "dropout factories" because of their high student dropout rates (Zuckerbord, 2007), you realize that for many students, becoming a productive citizen is a daunting challenge. Improving the literacy achievement of your child through the recommendations offered in this book will help him become a productive citizen (National Endowment for the Arts, 2007) as well as improve his performance on standardized tests.

On the other hand, some readers may think that the ideas contained in this book don't apply to them. Perhaps your child is an excellent standardized test taker, or maybe he has already been accepted into the university of his choice. Perhaps he is going into the military and already has passed the appropriate test. Then again, maybe you don't have any children, and you're just reading this book because you're bored. For those of you who are thinking that, you are wrong.

I can explain why you are wrong by relating to you an incident that actually occurred. A woman once said on television (during a discussion about school vouchers) that she didn't care about other people's children. She only cared about her child. I wish I had been in her presence. I would have told her that the child she did not care about could grow up to take the life of the child she did care about and love. So, I care about other people's children, not because I'm such a good person, but because I know the harm that other people's children can do.

Most of us don't live our lives in isolation, devoid of human contact with no one else around to affect, help, or unfortunately, hurt us. The academically underprepared students of today are possibly the societal misfits of tomorrow (Ferguson, 2005). We're all in this together, whether we want to be or not. Yes, we are our brother's keeper.

I once heard Oprah Winfrey say on her talk show that reading saved her life. Do not allow yourself to believe that it will do anything less for you and your child.

Appendix A
Questionnaire

1. Did your parents/guardian read stories to you prior to your entry into first grade?
2. If yes, approximately how many days/nights per week did your parents read to you?
3. How many books would you estimate had been read to you (or you read by yourself) by the time you entered first grade?
4. Did you voluntarily read for pleasure (reading not assigned by your teacher) when you were in elementary school?
5. Did you participate in summer reading programs, sponsored by your local library or other organizations, when you were in elementary school?
6. On average, approximately how many books did you read during the summer while you were in elementary school?
7. During middle school and high school, on average, approximately how many books did you read per calendar year? Don't include your school textbooks.
8. Is there anything else you can tell me about your reading experiences up to the age of 18?

Appendix B
The Jairrels' Reading Pledge

I pledge to do the following:
1. Encourage students in my class to read more by using Accelerated Reader or any other strategy that promotes reading.
2. Begin reading to my children from birth.
3. Read a book to my children who are 6 years old or younger every night/day. I realize that other parents may be reading 3 books or more a day to their children.
4. Take my younger children to the library on a biweekly basis, where we will check out at least 14 books each visit.
5. Encourage my children to enroll in a summer reading program sponsored by the local library or other organizations.
6. Encourage my children to read at least 50 books of 100 pages each during the summer or read for 30 minutes per day. If my children are reading very short (less than 15 pages, with illustrations on most of the pages) non-chapter books, they will read at least 180 books in a two-month period during summer vacation.
7. Encourage my older children to read for pleasure for at least 30 minutes per day each day of the year or encourage my older children to read at least 50 books (of at least 100 pages each) for pleasure during the academic year.
8. Encourage my children to participate in the Accelerated Reader Program or a similar program at school if available.
9. Share information from this pledge with at least one other parent.

_____

Signature   Date

Appendix C
Suggested Books

The following are books that children and youth might find interesting. I have only read three of the books on this list. Parents should always preview books to make sure there is no objectionable content.

Ages 14 and under

Brown, M.W. (2005). *Goodnight moon.* New York: Harper Collins.

This book is appropriate for children ages 4–8, although many mothers have read it to their infant children. It was originally published in 1947 and has been reprinted numerous times. It received excellent reviews on the Amazon Web site.

Curtis, C. P. (1999). *Bud, not Buddy.* New York: Delacorte.

This story is about an African American boy who runs away from his foster home. The book received the John Newbery Medal in 2000. The Newbery Medal is a prestigious award given each year to the author of an outstanding book for children.

Curtis, C. P. (1995). *The Watsons go to Birmingham - 1963.* New York: Delacorte.

Curtis, the author of *Bud, Not Buddy,* also wrote this story of an African American family that visits relatives in

Alabama in 1963. The book was a Newbery Honor winner, recognition given to outstanding books that did not receive the highest award, the Newbery Medal.

Green, T. (2007). *Football genius*. New York: Harper Collins.
Green is a former National Football League player. Green wrote this fictional book for boys, ages 10 to 14. The plot revolves around a 12-year-old protagonist who can correctly predict football plays.

Munsch, R. (1986). *Love you forever*. Willowdale, Ontario, Canada: Firefly Books.
This is my favorite children's book because of its message of unconditional love. It is aimed at children ages 4–8. I've only read it once, but I still remember the most important lines of the book. Whenever I say goodbye to my son, I quote a verse from this story.

According to reviews posted on the Amazon Web site, however, others seem to focus on a literal meaning of the text and illustrations and dislike the book immensely. Therefore, I reiterate that parents should preview all books to determine whether they are acceptable for their children.

Taylor, M.D. (2004). *Roll of thunder, hear my cry*. New York: Puffin.
This book is targeted to children ages 9–12 and is a John Newbery Medal winner. Taylor's book was first published in 1976. It's about a little African American girl and her family who live in the South during the 1930s.

Appendix C

Ages 15 and up

Davis, S., Jenkins, G., & Hunt, R. (2006). *The pact.* New York: Prentice Hall.

This is the true story of three African American males from the inner city who enter into an agreement to attend college and support each other. They were reared by single mothers, and one mother was a drug user. Today, two of them are medical doctors and the third is a dentist. One reviewer on the Amazon Web site said the book is suitable reading for teenagers and educators.

Davis, S., Hunt, R., & Jenkins, G. (2007). *The bond: Three young men learn to forgive and reconnect with their fathers.* New York: Riverhead.

The three African American male doctors who wrote *The Pact* also wrote this book. Their fathers, who were mainly absent from their lives, wrote chapters for the book. Mothers who are rearing children without assistance from the fathers may wish to read this book first to see whether it is suitable and inspirational for their children.

Harper, H. (2007). *Letters to a young brother: MANifest your destiny.* New York: Gotham.

Hill Harper is an African American magna cum laude graduate of Brown University and a cum laude graduate of Harvard Law School. He also has a master of public administration degree from the Harvard Kennedy School of Government. He is currently an actor and has appeared in several movies and television programs. He plays the role of Dr. Sheldon Hawkes on the television show *CSI: NY.*

This book discusses such topics as single parenthood and sexually transmitted diseases. It is aimed at young black men. Again, I emphasize that parents should read this book prior to giving it to their teenage children to read.

Harper, H. (2008). *Letters to a young sister: DeFINE your destiny*. New York: Gotham.

The author gives advice to young girls and women. One reviewer on the Amazon Web site said the book is appropriate for ages 12–24. The reviewers on the Amazon Web site gave the book an excellent rating.

References

A second chance. (2004, December 13). *America*, 191(19), 3–3.

ACT (2007). ACT high school profile report: The graduating class of 2007 National. Retrieved September 14, 2007, from http://www.act.org/news/data/07/pdf National 2007. pdf

Abdullah, H. (2007, October 30). Poor children now the majority in public schools in the South. *The Anniston Star*, pp. A1, A3.

About Tiger. Retrieved from www.tigerwoods.com September 26, 2007.

Adcox, S. (2008, March 30). South Carolina to offer cyber school full time in the fall. *The Anniston Star,* p. B7.

Albany fails again. (2008, April 9). *New York Times*. Retrieved April 11, 2008 from http://www.nytimes.com

Alexander, K.L., Entwisle, D.R., & Olson, L.S. (2007). Lasting consequences of the summer learning gap. *American Sociological Review, 72*, 167-180

Anderson, R.C., Wilson, P.T., & Fielding, L.G. (1986). Growth in reading and how children spend their time outside school. Technical Report No. 389. ERIC Document Reproduction No. 275 992.

Archwamety, T., & Katsiyannis, A. (2000). Academic remediation, parole violations, and recidivism rates among delinquent youths. *Remedial and Special Education*, 21(3), 161-170.

Ard, L., & Beverly, B.L. (2004). Preschool word learning during joint book reading: Effect of adult questions and comments. *Communication Disorders Quarterly*, 26(1), 17-28.

Armah, B. (2007). Read A Book. Added by Bomani. Retrieved October 22, 2007 from myspacetv.com

Arnold, R., & Colburn, N. (2006). From a distance. *School Library Journal*, 52(9), 32-32.

Arnold, R., & Colburn, N. (2007). Read to me! *School Library Journal*, 53(7), 25-25.

Arroyo, C.G. (2008, January 17). *The funding gap*. Retrieved January 19, 2008 from http://www2.edtrust.org/EdTrust/Press+Room/fundinggap07.htm

Associated Press. (2007, December 27). State-run school system could start handing out big bonuses. *Education Week*. Retrieved December 28, 2007, from http://www.edweek.org/ew/articles/2007/12/27/17apnola_web.h27.h...

Association for Library Service to Children. (2003). Born to read. [Brochure]. Chicago: American Library Association.

ASVAB Career Exploration Program (n.d.). Retrieved September 20, 2007 from http://www.asvabprogram.com/index.cfm?fuseaction=overview.test

References

The ASVAB Explained (n.d.). Retrieved September 20, 2007 fromhttp://www.military.com/ASAB/0,,ASVAB_ Explained 1html

Author Q & A. Retrieved June 23, 2007 from www.uncpress. unc.edu/interviews/h_williams_interview.htm

Barton, P.E., & Coley, R.J. (2007). The family: American's smallest school. Princeton, NJ: Educational Testing Service.

Benner, J., Beaudoin, K., Kinder, D., & Mooney, P. (2005). The relationship between the beginning reading skills and social adjustment of a general sample of elementary aged children. *Education and Treatment of Children, 28*(3), 250-264.

Birmingham approves low-cost laptop project. (2008, April 4). *eSchool News.* Retrieved April 14, 2008 from http://www.eschoolnews.com/news/top-news/?i=53412.

Bradley, R. H., Corwyn, R.F., McAdoo, H., & Coll, C.G. (2001). The home environments of children in the United States Part I: Variations by age, ethnicity, and poverty status. *Child Development, 72*, 1844-1867.

Bridgeman, B., & Wendler, C. (2005). Characteristics of minority students who excel on the SAT and in the classroom. Princeton, NJ: Educational Testing Service. Retrieved September 8, 2007 from www.ets.org/Media/Research/pdf/PICMINSAT.pdf

Brown, M.W. (2005). *Goodnight moon.* New York: Harper Collins.

Bus, A., Van IJzendoorn, M., & Pellegrini, A. (1995). Joint book reading makes for success in learning to read: A meta-analysis of intergenerational transmission of literacy. *Review of Educational Research, 65*(1), 1-21.

Bylut Ermitage, J., & Van Slurp, K. (2007). Reading, learning, relaxing, and having fun: Third-grade perspectives on sustained silent reading. *Illinois Reading Council Journal, 35*(2), 11-21.

Camara, W.J., & Schmidt, A.E. (1999). Group differences in standardized testing and social stratification (College Board Report No. 99-5). New York: The College Board.

Castillo, D. D. (2002). Decaying manuscripts reveal Africa's literate history. *The Chronicle of Higher Education,* A26-28.

Cech, S.J. (July 12, 2007). Much of achievement gap traced to 'summer slide.' *Education Week.* Retrieved July 13, 2007, from http://www.edweek.org/ew/articles/2007/07/12/43summer.h26html

Chandler, M.A. (2007, December 23). Students take quicker steps to literacy: Program targets achievement gaps. *The Washington Post,* p. LZ01.

Chaplin, D., & Capizzano, J. (2006). Impacts of a summer learning program: A random assignment study of

146

References

Building Educated Leaders for Life. (ERIC Document Reproduction Service No. ED 493056)

Chavez, S. M. (2008, April 24). Grand Prairie ISD seeks holidays for those passing TAKS. *The Dallas Morning News*. Retrieved April 29, 2008 from http://www. dallasnews.com

Christian, M. A. (2007, December 10). The legacy of Dr. Donda West. *Jet, 112*, 54-56.

Chute, E. (Monday, August 27, 2007). Experts agree: Reading must begin early and at home. Pittsburgh Post-Gazette. Retrieved August 29, 2007 www.post-gazette.com.

Clements, D.H., & Sarama, J. (2006). Your child's mathematical mind. *Scholastic Parent and Child, 14*(2) 30-39.

Clinton, H.R. (2003). *Living history*. New York: Simon & Schuster.

Cooper, H., & Valentine, J.C. (2001). Using research to answer practical questions about homework. *Educational Psychologist, 36*(3), 143-153.

Cosby, C.O., & Poussaint, R. (Eds.). (2004). *A wealth of wisdom: Legendary African American elders speak*. New York: Atria Books.

Cunningham, A.E., & Stanovich, K.E. (1998). What reading does for the mind. *American Educator, 22*(1-2), 8-15.

Dalessandro, S.P., Stilwell, L.A., & Reese, L.M. (2004). LSAT Performance with regional, gender, and racial/ethnic

147

breakdowns: 1997-1998 through 2003-2004 testing years. Newton, PA: Law School Admission Council, Inc.

Debell, M., & Chapman, C. (2006). Computer and Internet use by students in 2003. NCES 2006-065. Washington, DC: National Center for Education Statistics.

Douglass, F. (1845). Narrative of the life of Frederick Douglass, an American slave. Boston: Anti-Slavery Office. Retrieved June 23, 2007 from http://sunsite.berkeley.edu/literature /Douglas/Autobiography

Drakeford, W. (2002). The impact of an intensive program to increase the literacy skills of youth confined to juvenile corrections. *Journal of Correctional Education, 53*(4), 139-144.

Edmunds, K.M., & Bauserman, K.L. (2006). What teachers can learn about reading motivation through conversations with children. *Reading Teacher, 59*(5), 414-424.

Edwards, P.A. (1992). Involving parents in building reading instruction for African-American children. *Theory into Practice, 31*, 350-359.

Eppe Chamberlain, S. (2003). *Emergent literacy differences in Latino and African American children: Culture or poverty?* Unpublished master's thesis. University of Southern California, Los Angeles.

Fairclough, A. (2007). A class of their own: Black teachers in the segregated south. Cambridge, MA: Harvard University Press.

References

Farrell, E.F., & Hoover, E. (2007, October 12). At admissions conference, talk of standardized test, early decisions, and swag. *The Chronicle of Higher Education*, p. A35.

Federal Interagency Forum on Child and Family Statistics (2007). America's children: Key national indicators of well-being 2007. Washington, DC: U.S. Government Printing Office. Retrieved September 4, 2007 from www.childstats.gov/ Americaschildren/edu.asp

Ferguson, R.F. (2005). *Toward skilled parenting & transformed schools inside a national movement for excellence with equity.* Cambridge, Massachusetts: Harvard University. Retrieved May 12, 2008 from Harvard University, The Achievement Gap Initiative Web site: http://www.agi.harvard.edu Finder, A. (2005, September 25). Integrating schools by income a success in Raleigh. *The Anniston Star*. p. D6.

Fischgrund, T. (2004). SAT Perfect score: Seven secrets to raise your score. New York: Regan Books.

Fitzhugh, G. (1857). *Cannibals all! or slaves without masters.* Richmond, VA: A. Morris. Retrieved January 15, 2008 from http://reactor-core.org/cannibals-all.html

Flowers, T.A. (2003). Exploring the influence of reading for pleasure on African American school students' reading achievement. *High School Journal*, *87*(1), 58-63.

Fournier, R., & Tompson, T. (2008, September 20). Racial views steer some white Dems away from Obama.

Newsweek. Retrieved September 20, 2008 from http://www.newsweek.com/id/159929

Franklin, J.H., & Moss, A.A., Jr (2005). *From slavery to freedom: A history of African Americans* (8th ed.). New York: Alfred A. Knopf.

Freedman, S.G. (2008. March 26). A do-it-yourself SAT class, with no whining, or parents, allowed. *New York Times*. Retrieved July 20, 2008, from http://nytimes.com/2008/03/26/education/26education.html

Frontline (n.d.). *Secrets of the SAT: Interview with Claude Steele*. Retrieved October 4, 2007 from http://www.pbs.org/wgbh/pages/frontline/shows/sats/interviews/steele.html

Fryer, R.G., & Levitt, S.D. (2006). *Testing for racial differences in the mental ability of young children*. Retrieved May 12, 2008 from Harvard University, The Achievement Gap Initiative Web site: http://www.agi.harvard.edu

Gaines, P. (2007, September/October). Prosecutorial misconduct. *The Crisis*, 114, 13-14.

Gambrell, L.B. (2007). Reading: Does practice make perfect? *Reading Today*, 24(6), 16.

Gersten, R.K., Jordan, & Flojo, J.R., (2005). Early identification and interventions for students with mathematics difficulties. *Journal of Learning Disabilities*, 38(4), 293-304.

References

Glater, J.D., & Finder, A. (July 15, 2007). School diversity based on income segregates some. New York Times. Retrieved July 15, 2007 from http://www.nytimes.com/2007/07/15/education/15integrate.html?_r...

Glauber, B., & Poston, B. (2008, January 9). 33% of students here live in poverty: Milwaukee Schools feel impact on learning. *JSOnline Milwaukee Journal Sentinel.* Retrieved January 11, 2008 from http://www.jsonline.com/ story/index.aspx?id=705506.

Goff, P.A., Steele, C.M., & Davies, P.G. (2008). The space between us: Stereotype threat and distance in interracial contexts. *Journal of Personality & Social Psychology 94*(1), 91-107.

Gosa, T.L. (2007). Oppositional culture, hip-hop & the schooling of black youth. Retrieved May 18, 2008 from Harvard University, The Achievement Gap Initiative Web site: http://www.agi.harvard. edu

Gosa, T.L., & Alexander, K.L. (2007). Family (dis)advantage and the educational prospects of better off African American youth: How race still matters. *Teachers College Record, 109*, 285-321.

Gould, S.J. (1996). *The mismeasure of man.* New York: W.W. Norton.

Grandy, J. (1999). Trends and profiles: Statistics about GRE general test examinees by gender, age, and ethnicity. (2nd ed.). Princeton, NJ: Educational Testing Service.

Greenberg, E., Dunleavy, E., & Kutner, M. (2007). Literacy behind bars: Results from the 2003 National Assessment of adult literacy prison survey (NCES 2007-473). U.S. Department Of Education. Washington, DC: National Center for Education Statistics. Retrieved September 23, 2007 from http://nces.ed.gov/pubs2007/2007473_1.pdf

Guide for the College-Bound Student-Athlete. Retrieved September 20, 2007 from http://www.ncaa.org/library/general/cbsa/2007-08/2007-08_cbsa.pdf

Hall, E. (2001). Babies, books and 'impact': Problems and possibilities in the evaluation of a Bookstart Project. *Educational Review, 53*(1), 57-64.

Hanchett, T. Saving the south's Rosenwald Schools. Retrieved June 25, 2007 from http://rosenwaldplans.org/history.html

Henderson, M. (1996). Helping your student get the most out of homework. [Brochure]. Chicago: National Parent Teacher Association.

The Herbert S. Ford Memorial Museum: Research in progress-help needed-Rosenwald Schools in Claiborne Parish. Retrieved June 25, 2007 from http://ford.claiborneone.org/

Hermes, J.J. (2007, October 12). A plan to improve AP performance in Arkansas and other news from the states. *The Chronicle of Higher Education.* Retrieved

References

October 12, 2007, from http://chronicle.com/daily/2007/10/343n.htm

Hip Hop Press. (2007). Hip Hop Press Release. Retrieved October 4, 2007 from www.hiphoppress.com/2007/02/jasmine_guydeej.htm.

Hockenberger, E.H., Goldstein, H., & Hass, L.S. (1999). Effects of commenting during joint book reading by mothers with low SES. *Topics in Early Childhood Special Education, 19*(1), 15-27.

Home Box Office. (2002). Unchained memories: Readings from the slave narratives. New York: Bulfinch

Honig, A.S. (2004). Story time for baby. *Scholastic Parent & Child, 12*(2), 28-30.

Honig, A.S. (2007). Choosing great books for babies. *Early Childhood Today, 21*(4), 24-25.

Hoover, E. (2007, September 14). Admissions plan goes beyond numbers: Northeastern U's new scholarship program looks past grades and test scores to measure the potential of low-income students. *The Chronicle of Higher Education*, A25.

Human Rights Watch. (2003, April). *Incarcerated America*. Retrieved October 2, 2007 from http://www.hrw.org/backgrounder/usa/incarceration/

It's Hip to Read. (2007, October 15). *Jet, 112*, p. 23.

Ivey, S. (2007, November 30). The gift of reading: Teachers hope parents will give books for Christmas. *The Anniston Star,* pp. A1, A6.

Jackson, C.K. (2007, December 7). *A little now for a lot later: A look at a Texas advanced placement incentive program.* Retrieved December 14, 2007 from http://www.ilr.cornell.edu/cheri/wp/cheri_wp107.pdf

Jackson, L.A., von Eye, A., Biocca, F.A., Barbatsis, G., Zhao, Y., & Fitzgerald, H.E. (2006). Does home Internet use influence the academic performance of low-income children? *Developmental Psychology, 42*(3), 429-435.

James, S. (2008). Seattle teacher says tests kill learning. Retrieved April 29, 2008 from http://abcnews.go.com/print?id=4720675

Janvry, & A., & Sadoulet, E. (2004). *Conditional cash transfer programs: Are they really magic bullets?* Retrieved December 31, 2007 from http://are.berkeley.edy/~sadoulet/papers/ARE-CCTPrograms.pdf

Kaczor, B. (2008, April 7). State disciplines teachers who cheat on FCATs. *South Florida Sun-Sentinel.* Retrieved April 7, 2008, from http://www.sun-sentinel.com/news/local/florida/sfl-flffcat0407sbapr07,0,4520055,print.story

Keller, B. (2008, March 18). Studies link teacher absences to lower student scores. *EducationWeek.* Retrieved March

References

26, 2008 from http://edweek.org/ew/articles/2008/3/ 1928absentee.h27.html? print=1

Kobrin, J.L., Sathy, V., & Shaw, E. J. (2007). A historical view of subgroup performance differences on the SAT Reasoning Test. New York: The College Board. College Board Research Report No. 2006-5.

Krashen, S. (2006). Free reading. *School Library Journal*, *52*(9), 42-45.

Krashen, S. (2007). Let's not denigrate the "old view" of SSR. (Letter to the editor). August/September. *Reading Today*, *25*(1), 19-19.

Krueger, A.B. (2000, August 16). Summertime for pupils when forgetting is easy. *The New York Times*. Retrieved September 26, 2007 from http://www.nytimes.com/ library/financial/081700econ-scene.html

Lee, J., Grigg, W.S., & Donahue, P.L. (2007). The nation's report card: Reading 2007. Retrieved October 10, 2007 from http://nces.ed.gov/nationsreportcard/pubs/main 2007/2007496.asp

Lewontin, R., Rose, S., & Kamin, L.J. (1984). *Not in our genes*. New York: Pantheon.

Literacy Guide. (n.d.). Retrieved July 14, 2007 from http:// www.bankstreet.edu/literacyguide/early2.html

MacDonald, G. (April 26, 2006). Verdict's still out: Diversity vs. scores. *USA Today*, retrieved September 7, 2007, from Academic Search Complete database.

Making a profit. (2007, October 28). *Parade*, p. 10.

Mangan, K. (2008, January 18). Minority enrollment drops. *The Chronicle of Higher Education,* p. A22.

Mann, E.A., & Reynolds, A.J. (2006). Early intervention and juvenile delinquency prevention: Evidence from the Chicago Longitudinal Study. *Social Work Research, 30*(3), 153-167.

Marx, P. (2002, June 7)). Why we need the SAT. *The Chronicle of Higher Education,* B10-11.

McCague, J. (1972). The road to freedom. Champaign, IL: Garrard Publishing Company.

McLoughlin, J. A. & Lewis, R.B. (2008). *Assessing students with special needs.* Upper Saddle River, NJ: Pearson Prentice Hall.

McMackin, R.A., Tansi, R., & Hartwell, S. (2005). Proficiency in basic educational skills as related to program outcome and escape risk among juvenile offenders in residential treatment. *Journal of Offender Rehabilitation, 42*(3), 57-74.

Medina, J. (2008a, January 21). New York measuring teachers by test scores. Retrieved January 23, 2008 from http://www.nytimes.com/2008/010210nyregion 21teachers .html?_r=1&oref=slogin

Medina, J. (2008b, March 5). Next question: Can students be paid to excel? Retrieved March 26, 2008 from http://

REFERENCES

www.nytimes.com/2008/03/05/nyregion/05incentive
.html?_r=1&oref=slogin&ref=e.

Melton, C.M., Smothers, B.C., Anderson, E., Fulton, R., Replogle, W.H., & Thomas, L. (2004). A study of the effects of the accelerated reader program on fifth grade students' reading achievement growth. *Reading Improvement*, 41(1), 18-23.

Minorities mistrustful of each other, believe stereotypes, poll shows. (2008, January 7). *Jet, 112,* 12.

Mollin, G. (2005). Hoover Elementary turns to LeapFrog Schoolhouse. *T H E Journal, 33*(2), 48-48.

National Endowment for the Arts. (2007). To read or not to read: A question of national Consequence. (Research report No. 47). Washington, DC: National Endowment for the Arts. Retrieved November 19, 2007 from http://www.arts.gov/research/ToRead.pdf

National Reading Panel (2000). Teaching children to read. Washington, DC: National Institute of Child Health and Human Development. Retrieved September 22, 2007 from www.nichd.nih.gov/publications/nrp/findings.cfm

National Scientific Council on the Developing Child (2007). *The science of early childhood development.* Retrieved May 16, 2008 from http://www.developingchild.net

Nelson, T. (2007, December 8). 'Donuts with Dad' Program pushes reading: School also hosts 'Muffins with Moms.' Retrieved November 8, 2007 from www.coloradoan.com

Nisbett, R.E. (1998). Race, genetics, and IQ. In C. Jencks, & M. Phillips (Eds.)., The Black- White test gap. (pp. 86-102). Washington, DC: Brookings Institution.

Noble, P. (2003). Beyond the burning bus: The civil rights revolution in a southern town. Montgomery, AL: New South Books.

North, S., & Allen, N. (2005). A better beginning with books and libraries for western Australian babies. APLIS, *18*, 131-136.

Nussbaumer, J. (2006). The disturbing correlation between ABA accreditation review and declining African-American law school enrollment. *St. John's Law Review, 80,* 991-1005.

O'Neill, D. (2004). Narrative skills linked to mathematical achievement. *Literacy Today, 41*, 15-15.

The Online Teacher Resource (n.d.). Retrieved July 14, 2007, www.teach-nology.com/glossar/terms/e

Parrino, J. (2008, February 25). Web-based program gets students on reading kick. Retrieved February 26, 2008 from http://news.nky.com/apps/pbcs.dll/article?AID=/AB/20080225/NEWS0103/802250332.

Pearson Education Measurement Group (n.d.). Retrieved May 2, 2008 from http://www.pearsonedmeasurement.com/research/faq_2f.htm

REFERENCES

Perez, E. (2008, March 23). No-test option gives Lawrence a different look. Retrieved March 26, 2008 from htpp://www.jsonline.com/story/index.aspx?id=731278

Raikes, H., Luze, G., Brooks-Gunn, J., Raikes, H.A., Pan, B.A., Tamis-LeMonda, C.S., Constantine, J., Banks, L. B., & Rodriguez, E. T. (2006). Mother-child book reading in low-income families: Correlates and outcomes during the first three years of life. *Child Development*, *77*, 924-953.

Randolph County Heritage Book Committee. (2000). The heritage of Randolph County, Alabama. Clanton, AL: Heritage Publishing Consultants.

Read A Book Music Video Creators on CNN (2007). Retrieved October 22, 2007 from www.youtube.com.

Redondo, B., Aung, K., Fung, M., & Yu, N.W. (2008). *Left in the margins: Asian American students and the No Child Left Behind Act*. New York: Asian American Legal Defense and Education Fund. Retrieved May 9, 2008 from http://www.aadldef.org/docs/AALDEF_LeftintheMargins_NCLB.pdf

Report: Edwards' wife in anguish after affair. (2008. August 14). *The Anniston Star*, p. A3.

The Rosenwald Schools Initiative. (n.d.). Retrieved January 16, 2008 from http://www.rosenwaldschools.com/history.html#1.

Ryan, L.T. (2007, August 30). Tim Green tackles young readers: Ex-NFL player turned author is keen on books. *The Post-Standard*, pp. E1-2. Retrieved October 1, 2007 from www.timgreenbooks.com

Sabol, W.J., & Couture, H. (2008). Prison inmates at midyear 2007. Bureau of Justice Statistics Bulletin. Retrieved August 10, 2008 from http://www.ojp.usdoj.gov/bjs/pub/pdf/pim07.pdf

Schatmeyer, K. (2007). Hooking struggling readers: Using books they can and want to read. *Illinois Reading Council*, *35*(1), 7-13.

Schmidt, P. (2008, May 9). Researchers accuse selective colleges of giving admissions test too much weight. *The Chronicle of Higher Education*, p. A20-A21.

Schmidt, P. (2007, December 14). *Cash rewards for good AP scores pay off, study finds*. Retrieved December 14, 2007 from http://chronicle. com/news/index.php?id= 3635&utm_source=pm&utm_ medium=en

SPLC seeks justice for Louisiana's 'Jena 6.' (2007, Fall). SPLC Report, *37*, pp. 1, 5.

Start kids reading early, first lady says. (2002, November 2.). *Atlanta Journal Constitution*, p. G1.

Steele, C. 2004, May 3). Not just a test. *Nation*, 278, 38-41.

Sternberg, R. J. (July 6, 2007). Finding students who are wise, practical, and creative. *The Chronicle of Higher Education*, B11-12.

References

Straub, S. (2006, February/March). Exploring books with babies. *Scholastic Parent & Child*, 13, 48-48.

Sullivan, K.H. (2005). Benefits of baby talk. *Prevention*, 57(10), 147-148.

Teen book club-teenagers' attitudes toward reading. (2001, July 1). *American Demographics*. Retrieved October 27, 2007 from http://findarticles.com/p/articles/mi_m 4021/is_2001_July_1/ai_76574304.

Thompson, G.L. (2007). Up where we belong: Helping African American and Latino students rise in school and in life. San Francisco: Jossey-Bass.

Topping, K.J., Samuels, J., & Paul, T. (2007). Does practice make perfect? Independent reading quantity, quality and student achievement. *Learning and Instruction*, 17, 253-264.

Tracy, J. (2007, October 5). Bridging the gaps by banding together: Boys' clubs show MCAS successes. *Boston Globe*. Retrieved October 6, 2007 from http://www.boston.com/news/education/k_12/mcas/articles/2007/10/05bridging_the_gaps_by_banding_together/?page=1

Trotter, A. (2008, May 5). Online education cast as 'disruptive innovation." *Education Week*. Retrieved May 6, 2008 from http://www.edweek.org/ew/articles/2008/05/07/36disrupt_ep.he7.html?

U.S. Census Bureau (2007). Income, poverty, and health insurance coverage in the United States: 2006 Report.

U.S. Census Bureau: Washington, DC. Retrieved September 14, 2007 from http://www.census.gov/U.S. Department of Education. (n.d.). Digest of Education Statistics. Retrieved September 8, 2007 from http://nces.ed.gov/ programs/digest/d02/dt311.asp.

Vacca, J.S. (2004). Educated prisoners are less likely to return to prison. *Journal of Correctional Education, 55*, 297-305.

Virginia Historical Society. (n.d.) *The civil rights movement in Virginia: The closing of Prince Edward County's Schools.* Retrieved September 29, 2007 from http:// www.vahistorical. org/civilrights.pec.htm.

Waldron, C. (2007, October 1). Pupil reads 330 books. *Jet, 112,* 14.

Walker, A. (1982). *The color purple*. New York: Harcourt Brace Jovanovich.

Walker, A. (2008, March 28). Lest we forget: An open letter to my sisters who are brave. Retrieved May 3, 2008 from http://www.emorywheel.com/detail.php?n= 25344# comments

Washington, J. (2001). Early literacy skills in African-American children: Research considerations. *Learning Disabilities Research & Practice, 16*(4), 213-221.

References

Wasley, P. (2007, October 12). Home-schooled students rise in supply and demand. *The Chronicle of Higher Education*, pp. A1, A33-34.

Wiesen, J.P. (2006). Possible reasons for the black-white mean score differences seen with many cognitive ability tests: Informal notes to file. Retrieved October 4, 2007 from http://appliedpersonnelresearch.com/papers/adimpact.pdf

Yarosz, D.J. & Barnett, W.S. (2001). Who reads to young children?: Identifying predictors of family reading activities. *Reading Psychology, 22*, 67-81.

Yell, M.L. (2006). *The law and special education.* (2nd ed.). Upper Saddle River, NJ: Pearson Prentice Hall.

Your Baby Can Read (n.d.). Retrieved August 29, 2007 from http://infantlearning.com/research.html

Young people thrive on 30,000 words a day. (2008). Retrieved October 10, 2008 from www.youtube.com

Zuckerbord, N. (2007, October 30). 'Dropout factories.' *The Anniston Star*, p. A1, A3.

Notes

Notes

Notes